# ENDORSEMENTS

♦ • • • ♦

"We all yearn to hear and know in the core of our hearts that we are beautiful, blessed, and beloved. But this longing for the truth of our identity can only be satiated by a living relationship with God. The amazing thing is that through Christ we come to discover precisely that—we discover our identity as daughters of the unfathomably merciful and Good Father. Dr. Hackett's *Daughter by Design* is an essential resource for every woman seeking to discover the freedom of what it means to hold peace and joy in her core while she goes about her daily life. With decades of experience as a mother, a wife, a Doctor of Education in Psychology, and a daughter and disciple of God, Dr. MaryRuth Hackett has generously and prayerfully gathered all her treasures and brought them to bear on this most essential topic and pressing issue of our day—How do I live as a Daughter of the Heavenly Father?"

-Sr. Maria Kim-Ngan Bui FSB, *Daughter of St. Paul*

"Knowing who we *really* are is at the core of true freedom and happiness. Diving into our identity as a daughter of Christ will offer more joy than we could ever conceive. Take advantage of this book as it guides you toward a stronger understanding of who God created you to be!"

-Rachel Balducci, *author, speaker and co-host of The Gist on CatholicTV*

"With warmth and wisdom, MaryRuth Hackett delivers a much-needed personal retreat for women designed to restore our dignity and remind us of our identity. This book is an invitation to finally become the woman the Father had in mind from the beginning. Page by page, readers will reintegrate all the broken, scattered, lied-about parts of themselves into the place within where God waits to embrace His beloved daughter and welcome her home. A life of wholeness and integrity–that is God's deep desire for us as women. Grab a friend–or a group–and dive in!"

-*Claire Dwyer, Author,* This Present Paradise

"In a world fighting to define femininity, what it means to be a woman, and how to best be a mom, MaryRuth Hackett cuts through the noise and beautifully presents the idea that first we must understand who we are as daughters of the Creator of the universe. With a gentle hand and tender strength, MaryRuth helps us understand the feminine heart and the identity we must first accept and understand. This is an excellent book, needed now more than ever, and will be a gift to Catholic women everywhere."

-*Katie Prejean McGrady, award-winning author and host of The Katie McGrady Show on Sirius XM*

"If you are a Catholic woman whose efforts to grow in your faith are constantly frustrated by the demands of a busy life, Dr. Hackett's short, very readable book is for you. She writes not as a teacher from on high, but as a sister who draws upon the compelling stories of her own lived experience.

*Daughter by Design* is a well-written, insightful guide to finding the Heart of Christ in the midst of everyday, chaotic life. I consider it a modern-day, feminine version of Brother Lawrence's Classic, Practicing the Presence of God.

*Father Charlie Goraieb,*
*-Pastor, Our Lady of Mt Carmel, Tempe, AZ*

"Amid the dishes, diapers and daily dizziness, you may wonder- who am I? Dr. Hackett will help you discover your true identity and how to live that out day by day. Her writing is clear, concise and seeded with kernels of wisdom and practical applications. Her experience, strength and hope will be a great benefit to others, especially those who have given up or are just too frustrated with life to even care".

*Father John Bonavitacola,*
*-Pastor, Our Lady Of Lourdes, Sun City West, AZ*

"The moment I started reading the manuscript, I simply could not put it down as page after page revealed to me a powerful spiritual plan of action as well as a riveting life compass not only applicable to daughters but to sons as well. In fact, in my second round of reading the manuscript, the book spoke directly to me and my relationship with God. So, I highly recommend this wonderful book: *"Daughter by Design: Discovering your Identity as God's beloved Daughter"* to anyone seeking to discover and appreciate their God-given Identity. Thank you, Dr. Hackett, for this invaluable resource."

*-Father Robert Seraph Aliunzi,*
*Parochial Vicar, Our Lady of Mount Carmel, Tempe, AZ*

# Daughter by Design

*Discovering Your Identity as
God's Beloved Daughter*

## MaryRuth Hackett, PhD

© 2022 MaryRuth Hackett, PhD

All rights reserved. No portion of this book may be reproduced in any form without permission from the author, except as permitted by U.S. copyright law.

*Holy Bible: The Catholic Journaling Bible.* The New American Bible Revised Edition. Our Sunday Visitor Publishing, 2017.

ISBN: 979-8-9867948-0-8

Cover design and interior layout by Michael Fontecchio, Faith & Family Publications.

For more information or to order, visit MaryRuthHackett.com

Printed in the United States of America

*Mom and Dad, I am who I am because you first loved me, first believed in me and first taught me what it means to be God's beloved daughter.*

# CONTENTS

*Foreword* . . . . . . . . . . . . . . . . . . . . . . . . xi

*Introduction* . . . . . . . . . . . . . . . . . . . . . . 1

SECTION 1: IDENTITY . . . . . . . . . . . . . . 13

   Chapter 1: Imitation . . . . . . . . . . . . . . . . . 19
   Chapter 2: Integrity . . . . . . . . . . . . . . . . . 41
   Chapter 3: Intentionality . . . . . . . . . . . . . 53

SECTION 2: CHALLENGES . . . . . . . . . . . 65

   Chapter 4: Crosses . . . . . . . . . . . . . . . . . . 71
   Chapter 5: Comparison . . . . . . . . . . . . . . 85
   Chapter 6: Consistency . . . . . . . . . . . . . . 97

SECTION 3: PRAYER . . . . . . . . . . . . . . . . 109

   Chapter 7: Priorities . . . . . . . . . . . . . . . . . 115
   Chapter 8: Purposeful . . . . . . . . . . . . . . . 139
   Chapter 9: Practical . . . . . . . . . . . . . . . . . 149

Chapter 10: Conclusion . . . . . . . . . . . . . . . 163

*Citations* . . . . . . . . . . . . . . . . . . . . . . . . . 166

*Acknowledgments* . . . . . . . . . . . . . . . . . . 168

*About the Author* . . . . . . . . . . . . . . . . . . 170

# FOREWORD

♦ · · ·♦

It had been years into my spiritual journey that I finally realized what a patient and merciful God we have. After years of living a life in ministry, years of caring for my husband and multiple children, years of a "decent-enough" prayer life, I wasn't even aware of my own fragility and how much I was held by the magnitude of Our Lord's sovereign hand. Until everything came crashing down.

Then, you know, it all becomes painfully obvious. It's obvious when you experience physical, crippling suffering. It's obvious when you are hit with grief that shatters your world. It's obvious when you are brought face to face with wounds that you didn't even know were underneath the surface.

It's obvious, then, that we have a God who not only pours out love into our open wounds, leads us on a journey of healing, guides us into the waters of restoring peace, but a God who also creates us anew. Every single moment of every single day, our Lord longs to see His daughters becoming. Becoming what, you might ask?

Becoming His, I'm assured. Becoming who we were always made to be.

Being cleansed in the waters of His love, this is our birthplace as daughters of God. Where He purifies our hearts of our own sin and the world's evils, and where we finally see a true reflection of who we are: daughters of the Father.

I want to invite you on this journey with MaryRuth Hackett and me as we learn more about this daughterhood and who we are because of Whose we are. The Lord has given MaryRuth incredibly unique gifts which she has worked hard to specialize in, hone her craft, become a learner of life and our development. These giftings in MaryRuth, mixed with incredibly hard work and a heart for the Lord and women, will help guide us to slowly and prayerfully begin to uncover the layers of life that have taken us off course, so that we turn our gaze back to the Father and to His plan for our lives. She has done this for me personally many times, gently and kindly reminding me of my worth, my purpose, my goodness because I am His.

This book is not in your hands by accident. It is here for a reason. You are here for a reason. So take the first step with me, would you? Let's learn what it means that we are daughters of God, daughters created in His image, daughters by His design. This is why we were made, this is our purpose and our life's mission: to rest in the sovereignty of His hand and to finally become His.

*-Jenna Guizar*
Founder + Creative Director
Blessed is She

# INTRODUCTION

❖ ❖

*"Amen, I say to you, unless you turn and become like children, you will not enter the kingdom of heaven. Whoever humbles himself like this child is the greatest in the kingdom of heaven."*
Matthew 18:3-4

I told people that it didn't matter whether my baby was a boy or a girl. I had two small boys already and I knew how to do the Boy Thing. I argued that if I added another boy to our family then it would almost be a relief. The day I found out I was having a girl, my first daughter, I left the ultrasound appointment and headed straight to the mall - where I proceeded to buy the fluffiest, ruffliest dresses they had. And not just one. It was embarrassing. Nothing gender neutral would adorn this child. Apparently it *did* matter to me that I was having a daughter, and it left me feeling both thrilled and a little bit anxious too.

When she was just a baby, I consecrated her to Mary, because I was filled with a fear that something bad might happen to her. As she lay quietly wrapped in my arms in the empty church I asked the Blessed Mother to accept my little one as her own daughter, and I prayed for grace to fill in the gaps of my human weaknesses. My natural human ineptitude in raising my sons was somehow compensated for by my husband, but I felt the responsibility of raising this baby girl much more deeply. As a new Catholic I was still discovering what it meant to be a Beloved Daughter, how could I possibly pass on that understanding to my own innocent child?

Understanding our home forever with God our Father is such an essential component to understanding ourselves. I desire this understanding for both my daughters, but also for you, and quite honestly, I want to more deeply internalize this myself. We are set on a lifelong process to more fully realize our identity as someone who was created out of love, for love, to be loved forever.

The primary embodiment of who I am, and who you are, lies in our everlasting place, for we have been designed from eternity as God's daughter.

The role as daughter is the only role which will remain with us throughout life. It is not dependent upon the lives, love, or acceptance of others. It is not contingent upon our success or hard work. It can not be earned, and it cannot be lost. To live as a daughter means to continue to live in this uniquely positioned relationship with God our Father forever.

Neither our identity nor our purpose in life are found in our vocation or station in life, rather they are found through a relationship with God. Our identity as daughters is both discovered and fully realized daily, in particular through the opportunities we have to love and serve our Father. Our

# INTRODUCTION

purpose is found in how we live our lives as daughters of God, regardless of the circumstances.

There is no expectation of perfection as a daughter of the Perfect Father—we will not be loved as a function of how well we do any task or succeed in any area. As a reformed perfectionist, I take such comfort in this fact. We are loved for who we are, and who we are yet to become. We are molded and formed by our relationship with the Father. Although we grow through daily struggles and our interactions with others, holiness is born through our relationship with God.

As a daughter, we can find the peace and fulfillment that eludes us when we seek our identity elsewhere or through our human relationships. Too often we seek our worth from our personal relationships. Human relationships alone cannot sustain us or become our primary source of fulfillment. Even the most permanent of these relationships will change.

As my children grow and now begin to leave our home, I see how my role as mother will fade. Lord willing, I pray someday I may add the role of grandmother. One day, far in the future, I know I may too find that my title of wife is likely to be replaced with widow. We can not cling to these roles as our identity because they are transient. Our primary role is and has always been as Daughters of our Lord and King. We must enter into a relationship with others, joyfully striving to build love in our daily interactions and growing from the difficulties we endure without interpreting our struggles as a negative reflection of self worth. Our worth is found in our relationship with God the Father.

"Beloved, we are God's children now; what we shall be has not yet been revealed. We do know that when it is revealed we shall be like him, for we shall see him as he is."

1 John 3:2

Being God's beloved daughter begins with embracing the role and making a decision to invest what is necessary to foster an intimate relationship with Him. Now you may be thinking "easier said than done!" and I would agree with you completely. Which is why over the course of this book, we are going to work together to fully realize and internalize this truth so that we can be forever changed. For each of us, the process of discovering the daughter within consists of three aspects: striving for holiness not perfection, accepting our challenges as a way to grow in virtue, and cultivating time to grow in personal relationship with God. As we do this we develop the ability to live a more authentic life using our gifts with confidence.

Accepting your role as the daughter of the Lord means recognizing your unique gifts so that you may use them for God's glory.

- It means living intentionally in community with those whom He has placed in your life.
- It means growing through your struggles and letting each challenge draw you closer to Him as He strengthens you.
- It means picking up your cross and uniting your life with His through prayer.

Understanding how we are uniquely designed as God's daughter starts with developing a self-awareness of our strengths and weaknesses. In order to do this, we must understand our own individual gifts and how to use those gifts with confidence, releasing expectations of perfection, and striving towards holiness.

Secondly, we must learn that our challenges are part of our path to holiness. We all have individual crosses to bear, and it is easy to fall into despair when we compare our lives to those of others. Yet it is in the challenges that we have our opportunity for the most growth, and it is in the daily frustrations of life that we are presented the continual and almost constant opportunity to do His will. Peace does not come from our circumstances, it comes from within and above. Even in the most peaceful of situations, some of us feel angst or anxiety because we lack a trust in the Lord. Trust is slowly cultivated through prayer.

In order to fully discover the daughter within, we must develop the space in our life to have regular conversations with the Lord. He is there for us, but in our busy moments, we don't always seek Him. In the noise of everyday life, we can't always hear Him. It is my desire that through this study you will develop the ability to find Him in the struggle of everyday life and learn to use your individual gifts in cooperation with His grace to respond in holiness and love regardless of the circumstances. Now I don't promise that you will be able to do it perfectly all the time because I still struggle, but you will gain a competency that you can practice throughout life.

# INTRODUCTION

## How to Retreat in Everyday Life

*"Wouldn't it be a pity to not understand ourselves?"*
St. Teresa of Avila

This book is a self-study that is going to encourage you to slow down, to read, and to reflect. Racing through the chapters and skimming over the questions will not lead you to the awareness of who you are in the eyes of the Lord or provide you with the peace or the relationship with God that you seek. This is a journey rather than a book you can skim for the main points. I am a psychologist after all! Each section has questions to help you move the concept from the theoretical to the practical. When you find yourself without an answer, make a note of it. I invite you to come back to that question in your next prayer time. Think of it while you go through your tasks of the day. Your answers to these questions may change over time as you grow in your relationship with the Lord and come to more fully understand how He knows and loves you.

In the first chapter of Mark, Jesus was baptized by John, and then He immediately went into the desert before beginning his public ministry. The actual terminology used is, *"At once the Spirit drove him out into the desert"* (Mark 1:12). In other words, Jesus Himself escaped into solitude. So too should we take time to escape the world around us, even if it is just in small bits of time. You don't need to run off to the desert! Simply find some way, some place where you can be uninterrupted for a little while.

As you begin, take a few deep breaths, get comfortable, and relax! Our God is the God of Peace, not chaos (Philippe, 1991). He is always with us of course, but He is so much easier to find in peace.

And let's take a moment to acknowledge that you've already taken the first two steps to learning how to retreat: You purchased this book, and you have found a little snatch of time to read. I love celebrating the little things, so let's just celebrate that for a moment. It probably wasn't easy to do either of those things. We have a million excuses for why we don't take the time to invest in ourselves. But I want you to know that you, more than anything, are worth the investment.

You are a daughter of God the Lord of All, and He desires that you know Him better.

- He desires that you learn to see yourself in the way He sees you.
- He desires that you recognize the gifts and talents He has endowed you with.
- He wants you to cooperate with the abundance of grace He is unleashing over you.
- He loves you and wants you to discover your place as His beloved daughter.

This book is purposefully short and divided into sections that can be digested slowly. You are given scripture to ponder, questions to prod, opportunities to think about yourself and your relationship with the Lord. My hope is that everything you read and everything you journal or reflect upon will help

## INTRODUCTION

you to understand more deeply that who you are is defined by Whose you are.

And you, my sister in Christ, are God's.

Let me add this too: human beings are creatures of habit and if we can develop a habit of prayer and study, we are more likely to follow through with the intention. For example, during Lent and Advent, I typically add an additional little prayer time in the morning before the house wakes up. It is hard, but it is a short time I set aside for that special liturgical time. If you are hoping to add something, and follow this text through to the end, you need to make it an intentional practice each day, in whatever way it works best for you. This will enable you to persevere in this personal retreat.

For some of you that may mean you make the most of many little snatches of time. Perhaps you do this study for fifteen minutes in the morning, or you take the first thirty minutes of a nap-time or a lunch break. It can be done in shorter segments or all at once over a longer time of personal retreat.

The important thing is to have a plan and stick to that plan. Your plan for how-to-do this self-study does not have to be a lasting plan because thankfully this book is small in scope, so think big!

How can you make the time for this in your busy life? When and how are you going to make time for this? Make a commitment to yourself and write it down on the next page.

# INTRODUCTION

Once you have your special time set aside, make that time different. What I mean is, before each section, take a moment to quiet your mind. This is intended to be more like a retreat rather than an instruction manual, so you need to approach it differently than you would another type of text. Maybe light a candle, lower the lights, and definitely try to relax. If you are working with only a certain amount of time, set your timer. Turn off phone alerts. Maybe you quiet the house or you need a little music to help drown out the other noises. Sit in a peaceful place, with a view of the crucifix if possible. Escape to a place that is free from laundry or other chores or distractions. I envision some of you in your home alone, but maybe you are with a small group of other women. Maybe you are in your car working on this while your children have activities. Whatever it is, make that time intentionally special. And the easiest way to make anytime special? Simply invite the Holy Spirit to be with you.

The time spent reading and reflecting on the chapters that follow should feed you as you begin to align your heart with the Lord. Now let us get started aligning our hearts to His!

> *"If we are open to the love of God – a love that is revealed to us through the love we share with one another – then we will discover who we really are."*

Hart, 2013

God loves you and created you to be in relationship with Him. Even though you aren't perfect, even though you have sinned, Jesus Christ became man, took on all our sin, conquered death and rose again. Let yourself be restored to a relationship with God through Jesus Christ. He desires nothing less for you.

God's love for us is more than enough to make up for our weaknesses. But like all relationships, a relationship with God requires effort from us. I invite you now to deepen your relationship with Our Father, and come to greater self-awareness, yourself, and live the life you were created to live as His beloved.

◆· · ·◆

*Lord, My Father,*
*I desire to know You and love You more deeply.*
*Help me to see myself as You see me.*
*Help me to learn and grow in Your love. Help me*
*to commit time and energy to nurture to a deeper*
*relationship with You.*
*Amen.*

# SECTION 1
# IDENTITY

"See what love the Father has
bestowed on us
that we may be called the
children of God."

1 John 3:1

We are created to be in relationship with God. We are created to love and be loved. The purpose of our creation is tied deeply to who we are as daughters of God the Father.

As St. John points out, the Father bestowed love on us relationally as His children. We are His. If we fail to accept the role of His daughter as primary, we will continue to struggle to fully understand ourselves. We are created to love the Lord and be loved by Him first of all–or we will be forever lost.

Although at times we let other roles take priority over our first role and responsibility as daughters, we must remember that we are above all else daughters of the Creator of the universe. We were created for a unique purpose to love and serve Him, our Beloved.

Everything we do and every other role we occupy should be informed and fed through this primary relationship with God the Father.

What does it actually mean to be a daughter?

It seems simple, but it is worth asking, because that role has changed for us all as we moved from childhood to adulthood. At one time, being a daughter meant complete dependence on our parents, but now as an adult it may mean serving them as their need for help becomes greater. As our role changes with our earthly parents, we remain their daughters as long as we retain a relationship with them. Our role may change, but the relationship of love can be the same. And we can't have a relationship with someone from whom we are estranged.

As daughters of God, we also must seek to remain in relationship with the Lord. That is primary to understanding and internalizing the role of the daughter. There will be times when we call to Him for aid, times when we struggle with anger or disappointment in His response, times when we realize we must give of ourselves in order to help others out of love for Him. All the while, we strive to remain in relationship with Him, open to His guidance, protection and love.

*"We love because he first loved us."*
1 John 4:19

I know it is harder in practice than theory. The day-to-day grind can make it easy to become distracted by life. But as we receive God's love and spend time with Him, deepening our dependence on Him and establishing our identity as His daughter, we come to understand something else, too. We come to know our unique gifts.

# INTRODUCTION

When my youngest entered all-day kindergarten, I was suddenly met with the reality that I had created a life as a professional volunteer.

Even prior to having children I knew that I wanted to be a stay-at-home mom. I had earned a PhD in Educational Psychology and studied human development academically for over a decade. I was determined to be the primary caretaker for my children throughout their life. Yet I was working a heavy, at least part-time schedule each day volunteering. I served on the school board, was a class mom, helped plan and run Vacation Bible School, started a consignment sale and mother-daughter tea and started two ministries at our parish as well.

If something needed doing, I was your girl. Anytime someone asked for help I said "Yes!" because somehow I valued that work as greater than the duties of motherhood. I was seeking personal value from the gratitude I received from others.

Some of those roles used my unique gifts, but many of them did not. I quickly became exhausted and burned out and yet spent little time growing internally in the spiritual life.

When you know your gifts and use them effectively, you'll be less likely to be pulled by the endless needs or wants of others. You will be deliberate about what you say yes to and what you say no to, allowing time and energy for this all-important relationship with our Loving Father. Although it is in our nature to serve those we love, we must know how to best serve *Him* in each situation and live with greater intentionality. After all, our very capacity to love others is rooted in our ability to receive God's love and grace. In the next few chapters we will explore our own unique design and how we can continue to grow to be the daughter God invites us to be.

Chapter 1

◆ ⋯ ◆

# IMITATION

*Brethren, join in following my example, and observe those who walk according to the pattern you have in us.*
Philippians 3:17

It was our typical late-afternoon routine in those early years of parenthood. I sat as the boys played around the water's edge and the baby slept in her stroller. We loved our afternoon walks. They were the perfect antidote for the restlessness of those hours just before dinner. The park was only a few blocks away, there were no busy streets to be crossed, and not only did it have a pond, but it had ducks.

We live in the desert where ducks and ponds are not natural to our environment and I was delighted to have a park with a pond nearby. While the boys played on the rocks and climbed the trees I settled into the damp grass. I was cognizant of the growing moisture seeping into my jeans, but was also too tired and content to care. Also I knew it would make the boys laugh when I got up and they discovered my wet pants. (Potty humor is something the boys never seem to grow out of!)

The ducks slowly made their way over to me. Two adults and two little ones. I looked on as they made their nonlinear journey closer to the shore, then swirled back, the parents evaluating if I had any bread and the baby ducks simply following.

I watched, fascinated.

I love ducks. They may actually be my favorite animal. I love watching them swim around peacefully on the glassy water while their little flippers paddle under the surface. I love the way they waddle on the shorelines. I love the way the little ducklings cluster around the mama, watching her, learning from her, imitating her.

Ducks are well known to imprint upon their mother at birth. The mama ducks sit on her clutch of eggs for weeks. She protects them from predators, keeps them warm, and remains close by when the eggs start to crack. Once the ducklings emerge from the eggs, they look to their mother. They *imprint*, which means they form a deep and lasting attachment to their mama duck.

This imprinting is the basis for how a duck learns to be a duck. In cases where the mother duck is absent and the duck imprints on another animal, it does not always result well. Ducks learn how to actually be themself by imitation.

# IMITATION

Similarly, human babies also learn much by imitation. Recently, I was watching my adult brother interact with his baby. When my brother smiled at the baby, she smiled in return. When he did raspberries with his lips, his sweet little girl tried to do the same thing. When he opened his mouth in surprise, she imitated him. I was struck by how we learn so much not just about the world, but about how we are to act within the world, by imitating others. It's part of the way we were designed.

In St. Paul's letter to the Philippians, he writes "join with others in being imitators of me, brothers, and observe those who thus conduct themselves according to the model you have in us." (Philippians 3:17). Note he says "according to the model you have in us". We have a model for behavior we are called to imitate.

We imitate virtuous actions because we have the desire in our hearts placed there by God. If we believe in Christ, then we should imitate actions in accordance with those beliefs. We have no shortage of lives to imitate in the vast communion of saints in our Catholic faith—and because our imitation is founded on our love of God, when we imitate their lives, it is not being fake. If we believe what we say is true, and if we act out of love, our actions are authentic.

St. Paul sends a similar message in his letter to the Ephesians in chapter 5 when he writes, "So be imitators of God, as beloved children, and live in love, as Christ loved us and handed himself over for us as a sacrificial offering to God for a fragrant aroma" (Ephesians 5:1-2).

*Who are your models of everyday holiness?
What can you learn from them?*

# IMITATION

Sometimes we recognize within ourselves some certain gift, but we fail to act because we don't think we are ready yet or holy enough. We doubt ourselves, our capabilities, even our adequacy.

We also can suffer from what psychologists call *imposter syndrome* where we don't think we are good enough to teach or preach to others. When we start to use our gifts, but lack trust or confidence, we can feel like impostors. What would that have looked like if St. Paul had more fear than faith? He could have been called the biggest imposter in the Bible. Yet St. Paul asks us to be imitators of him as someone completely confident in God's call. When it comes to spiritual life, there are no imposters. There are hypocrites–those who SAY one thing and do another–but if you are an imitator of Christ, and of Paul, your actions are paramount, not your words.

Your intentions also count. This is a lesson I focus on so much with my children. Did you *mean* to do what you just did? Did you *mean* to hurt me with those words? Did you *mean* to knock over that plant? Being thoughtful and intentional about our actions is so important.

St. Paul continues, "Keep on doing what you have learned and received and heard and seen in me. Then the God of peace will be with you" (Philippians 4:9). Notice that he tells them to do what they have seen in him. We have models of good and holiness around us in and throughout scripture. We have models of holiness in the lives of the saints. And there are good and holy people who live and breathe and work around us every day as well.

*What do you want your actions to say about you?*

*Think back on your week. What did your actions actually say about you? Our past doesn't define us, but our actions can be defining of us when they reflect our heart's intentions. In what ways did you glorify God through your actions and when did you fail to do so?*

_____

_____

_____

_____

_____

_____

♦ ♦ ♦

Lord, My Father,
Open my eyes to the models of goodness in my life. Let my actions speak of love. Forgive me for the times they have failed to do so.

## Mary, Our Perfect Model

In his apostolic letter, *Mulieris dignitatem,* Pope Saint John Paul II called women to embrace their Feminine Genius and outlined four areas where women are uniquely created to nurture and sustain human life:

- Receptivity–both a giving and receiving of life and love.
- Sensitivity–being able to see and understand the needs of the human heart which then allows us to respond with love.
- Generosity–when paired with receptivity and sensitivity allows us to value the individual in such a way which opens us to giving freely.
- Maternity–is the capacity for physical and spiritual motherhood.

We see these four areas perfectly embodied in Our Blessed Mother, and so we should take Mary as our model of womanhood. How we personally model that will take into account our own gifts, and thus we will all model her differently. Your ways of serving likely look very different than mine and look different than those of Mother Mary, for we are each designed to be and do something different for this world.

Our unique dignity encapsulates all of the gifts we have to offer.

For a while, there was a really popular phrase, *What Would Jesus Do?* or *WWJD*. I would see it on necklaces or bracelets. Kids had it printed across their shirts. It was a reminder to reflect on our own actions and respond in a way that Jesus would have. I think if women could reflect more on Mary, they would have a particularly good model for what it means to be a woman. She is the ultimate Mama, but she was first an obedient Daughter.

## Your Fiat

During Advent a few years ago, I prayed for a specific direction regarding my vocation. I was looking for a word to guide me through the year, and the word I kept hearing in my heart was *fiat*. I was not even sure what the word meant, but it kept coming up in prayer and in the quiet moments. So, trying to be obedient to God's inspirations, I looked up its meaning. Traditionally the word *fiat* means dictate or decree. As Catholics we often hear about Mary's *Fiat*. I took the word to mean more than just a decree, but rather a feeling of acceptance or welcoming even to a request.

I accepted as my *fiat* to be more open and accepting of the desires of the Lord. I wanted to say Yes to Him. I wanted to be more receptive to His work in my life. I knew I had gifts to use, but I had been reluctant to break from the comfortable in order to pursue new avenues of evangelizing.

God shook me out of the comfortable with a simple phone call. The call came as I was chatting with a group of friends in the kitchen. "Father" appeared on the screen. I had never had a priest call me before. He was the only Father I had saved in my contacts and he was a fairly recent addition. We had begun working together with a ministry for which he was the chaplain, but we had never really chatted outside of the work environment so I was intrigued.

I stepped into a quieter part of the living room to take the call and his excitement was electric even through the phone. "Have you ever considered doing a podcast?" he asked. I explained that I had actually considered it, but as a mom with four kids at home I just didn't have the bandwidth to learn a whole new technology. A friend had got me started blogging, and another one had created my website, but all I knew how to do was think, research, and write. Father responded with, "What if we take care of all the technology, and you just show up to record?"

Now to fully appreciate this invitation, I have to give you just a little more backstory.

When I was in graduate school my mentor and advisor had planted a seed. He told me that although he knew I was committed to be a stay-at-home mom, he predicted I would actually remain an educator. Dr. Ridley said I would find a way to continue to educate others about how the human mind grows and develops throughout life but through the lens of faith. He was confident I would do this after I had earned my PhD and my home and heart was full of children. He knew I had the passion and God would show me the path. He said I would bridge the gap between what academics know and what is practiced in the home, and do it without ignoring my faith.

The Vicar for Evangelization for my diocese, or simply "Father" in my contacts, was now calling me on a random

Thursday night to ask me to start a parenting podcast for my diocese. Father Parks was asking me to do what Dr. Ridley had predicted, and the diocese was going to do whatever they could to make it happen. After taking it to prayer and discussing it with my husband and children, I returned the call and soon added Podcast Host to my volunteer vita.

But note however, that I didn't just yell yes. I had to take the invitation and really sit with it in prayer. As much as I would have loved to just spout off a resounding AWESOME, I knew that a podcast would ultimately mean my oversharing family stories and events. My family's privacy needed to be considered and their opinions consulted as well. Similarly, simply shutting off any possibility of the project in an attempt to exercise an over-abundance of caution, wouldn't have been prudent either because it lacked courage.

When we show both courage and prudence in our response to the Lord's invitations, we are able to give an answer that is more congruent with our life purpose and the character we are continuing to develop. This helps us to remain true to our identity as His trusting daughter as we step into a role which we were designed to take.

What is often required is an outward, intentional– and thoughtful– "Yes" to cooperate with the Lord's will in our life.

This can be called *intentionality of action*, and when it is directed towards service to the Lord, it helps promote integrity because it aligns us with the purpose, duties, roles and responsibilities to which He has uniquely called of us. This is the precise and personal way we've been created to live out the feminine gifts of receptivity, sensitivity, generosity, and maternity.

In what way do you need to say Yes to the Lord? Is there something you have been neglecting to accept or something that you've accepted too rashly that may not be His Will? Fill in the rest of this sentence:

*Lord, as Your obedient daughter, trusting in your mercy and love, please help me to*

_____

_____

_____

_____

_____

_____

Our Blessed Mother perfectly encapsulates surrender to the Lord. She is also a beautiful example of receptivity, sensitivity, generosity and maternity. Even if you are not an earthly mother, these four aspects of the feminine genius are all parts of our

## IMITATION

identity as daughters and part of the way we can reflect the virtues of Our Heavenly Mother.

Pope Saint John Paul II wrote of the Blessed Mother in *Redemptoris Mater*:

> "It can thus be said that women, by looking to Mary, find in her the secret of living their femininity with dignity and of achieving their own true advancement. In the light of Mary, the Church sees in the face of women the reflection of a beauty which mirrors the loftiest sentiments of which the human heart is capable: the self-offering totality of love; the strength that is capable of bearing the greatest sorrows; limitless fidelity and tireless devotion to work; the ability to combine penetrating intuition with words of support and encouragement" *(Catholic Church, 1987).*

Mary offers an example of self-donative love, a quiet strength in sorrow, a devotion to her family, and a balance of "penetrating intuition with words of support and encouragement." We also are each created to love and to do something which will make this world a little better. We are designed to help others on their journey to holiness, just as so many others are helping us.

Take a moment and jot down the ways in which you are able to intentionally live out the Feminine Genius. I think this is a hard question, so I will go first and give you my answers.

Receptivity: I am a good host. I try hard to bring people together and help them to feel welcome and loved. I am also (usually) open to growth and critique. I want to receive direction and instruction so that I can continue to live as my best self. Sensitivity: I can tell when someone is in need of extra love or attention. I listen well. Generosity: I strive to be giving of my time as I serve my family. I am willing to share what I have. I am generous with my compliments and strive to find the good in others. Maternity: I love to take care of people. I love to bring life to thoughts and ideas and share those with others, helping them to grow and understand themselves better.

Now it is your turn!

**Receptivity:**

_____

_____

_____

**Sensitivity:**

_____

_____

_____

IMITATION

## **Generosity:**

## **Maternity:**

♦ ♦ ♦ ♦

Lord, My Father,
Give me the strength to say Yes. Grant me the
confidence to live more like Mother Mary. Help me
to develop a personal internal awareness of my
embodiment of the Feminine Genius.
Amen.

## Perfection

As we begin to discover our various strengths and weaknesses and God's call on our lives, it is important to recognize that we are not on a perpetual self-improvement plan by which we hope to someday seek perfection. We are seeking a greater sense of peace and deeper understanding throughout our life rather than perfection.

We don't have to be perfect to use our gifts. Only surrendered.

We can say we want to bring glory to God through our actions, but sometimes we fail to actually act because we fear failure and rejection. We worry that we aren't good enough to do what God has asked us to do. Our fear of imperfection can paralyze us.

Are you seeking peace in your life or striving for perfection?

The peace that comes from the Lord does not come from circumstances, but rather from acceptance of the love from God and certainty in His plan for our life. Are you seeking peace in your life or striving for perfection? Maybe you are simply trying to survive the day to day? Being intentional about our Yes to the Lord, and saying yes with a trusting heart will bring peace.

This awareness is important because perfection is a real obstacle to trusting surrender and finding true peace. For perfectionists, their worth, or feelings of worth, is contingent upon some outcome of success or failure. For them, nothing less than perfection is considered a success. We can see why perfectionism is also highly correlated with anxiety and depression!

But these unrealistic expectations of ourselves—and we all have them sometimes, perfectionist or not—are toxic to both our self-worth and our relationships. It is based on a concept of self-reliance which tells us that if we just can be good enough, or work hard enough, we won't need anyone else and everything will be okay.

On the surface, perfectionism seems like one of those faults that is closely aligned to a strength. It is a characteristic one might strategically mention in an interview as their biggest "fault"—a way of communicating to their possible future employer that they are a solid person who can be depended upon.

In reality, perfectionism can undermine and erode one's relationships with others, inhibit one's ability to take risks and try new things, and even affect one's very acceptance of self and ability to surrender to the will of God. The perfectionist strives not just to be the best and most authentic version of herself, but rather to be free from fault, free from failure, free from criticism or correction.

Perfectionism can permeate and suffocate everyday life. Decision making, interactions with others, expectations of loved ones, daily life satisfaction, and even our prayer life can be tainted by an unhealthy drive to excel in everything. Friendships can be fractured by disappointment. Conflict can be avoided and then erupt explosively. Exhaustion can be a constant companion because there is always more to be done, always improvements to be made. For the perfectionist, the emphasis is always on the outcome or the finished product rather than the process, the joy of the activity, or the learning that has taken place. It's a broken, impoverished way to exist.

What is underneath perfectionism?

It is an undercurrent of self-reliance which extends beyond healthy independence. The perfectionist strives to be all and therefore needs no one. After all, she reasons, others are flawed and therefore a disappointment in the end. The perfectionist frequently expects to be able to operate as a self-contained entity in the area in which she operates. Her success is because she earned it through her efforts. Her failures on the other hand are often because of the system or other people's flaws.

I've observed that:

- The perfectionist tends to be justice rather than mercy oriented.
- The perfectionist is self-reliant.
- The perfectionist is judgmental of others and of the self, but can be defensive when critiqued. Everything is personal.

My biggest struggle with perfectionism, I've come to realize, is in the area of relationships. There is a misnomer that as we get older, relationships become easier. My adult relationships have given me far more difficulty than the relationships of my childhood years. And yet now, in the middle years of my life, I am slowly beginning to understand that the difficulty in relationships is not due to the imperfections of myself or others. The failure lies rather in my need for self-reliance and desire to control the outcome of the experience, rather than accept a childlike dependence on the Lord, accept God's mercy for myself, and extend love rather than judgment towards others. And so I am trying with each passing year to grow in this area.

The awareness of this problem in my life arose in my first confession when I was in my 30s and was coming into full communion with the Church. The sweet (but very direct) old priest Father Bernie was patient with my litany of sin accumulated through my early years of adulthood. Then he very pointedly responded, "So when people don't meet your expectations you just drop them from your life?"

Ouch.

Every ounce of me wanted to respond with an arrogant denial and yet the recognition brought with it an odd sort of peace. I had to admit that he had summed up a few relationships quite well. I was frustrated when others failed. I took upon myself the role of judge and jury condemning our relationship. Many years later now, as a mother with young adult children, I continually ask for the grace to love more than I judge and to recognize that my children need love more than anything. I hope I will always be in a position to offer them guidance, but that must look different at different stages of life. I must be willing to adapt my role and response to what they need–which is not necessarily what I want to give at the time.

The cure for perfectionism is not to stop caring or trying, but rather to surrender your concerns to the Lord, and give him control over the situation. You still have to show up and do the hard work, but you do so at His command and invite Him into the situation. Maybe it is a difficult relationship to which you have been clinging and God really wants you to let go, or maybe it is a professional role you are trying to grow in and you are simply impatient with yourself. Maybe it is a challenge you have decided not to take because you are scared of failing. Clinging to something, being discouraged, or giving up won't lead to success. Success comes when we surrender it to the Lord and then listen to His response on how we are to proceed.

*In what area of your life are you clinging to your own self-reliance or striving for perfection rather than letting go?*

# IMITATION

*When have you failed to act because you were scared of an imperfect result or failing altogether?*

No one is like you; you were made for a distinct purpose in this world. Think about that for a moment. We will have aspects of our lives as daughters of the good and loving Father that we have in common with others. Yet we were created uniquely for a distinct purpose and, through prayer, God will reveal that purpose to us in due time. You were designed intentionally by the Creator of Heaven and Earth. He created you differently than He created anyone else, and no one else in the world is like you. No one is like you, so no one can give in the way you can give. He has endowed you with a bouquet of gifts that no one else has.

♦ · · ·♦

*Lord, My Father,*
*Thank you for creating me just as I am.*
*Thank you for this mind and body.*
*Thank you for these gifts.*
*Thank you for me.*
*Amen.*

Chapter 2

## INTEGRITY

*"Be doers of the word and not hearers only, deluding yourselves. For if anyone is a hearer of the word and not a doer, he is like a man who looks at his own face in a mirror. He sees himself, then goes off and promptly forgets what he looked like. But the one who peers into the perfect law of freedom and perseveres, and is not a hearer who forgets but a doer who acts, such a one shall be blessed in doing what he does."*
James 1:22-25

We all have notions of what it means to live a life of integrity. But what does that mean, exactly? It means to persevere, that our word is our bond, and that we hold fast to commitments. It means that we aren't easily tempted or swayed to change our mind when offered an easier but less righteous path. It means we choose to do the right thing even when we do not feel like doing so. I don't know about you, but that's how I want to live my life. I want to be a woman of integrity.

Having integrity means acting according to strong moral principles and being honest. If we call ourselves Christian, this basically means acting in accordance with God's Laws for our lives. Living out the virtues every day, and being both charitable and trustworthy, is essential to the Christian life.

When we talk about integrity, we really are talking about two things: sound moral judgment and being complete or whole. I challenge you to think of integrity of the person, as referring not only to morality, but *wholeness* that encompasses our morality. I love the definition of integrity as wholeness because it refers to us coming into our whole person. We are accepting our whole being, our entire identity. We are not segmenting ourselves and defining ourselves by one role or another. We don't act as a mother in one setting, act like a diva when we are with certain friends, as a boss lady in a third context, and as a daughter in another.

We are the same person in every setting.

*When you think of integrity, which individuals come to mind?*

# INTEGRITY

*What sort of integrity have they shown?*

_____

_____

_____

_____

*What type of a woman do you want to be?
What are the virtues you recognize in yourself
that you want to be more salient? How do
you want to be remembered by others?*

_____

_____

_____

_____

As daughters of God, living a life of integrity means we strive towards the goal of living authentically in our purpose of both wholeness and holiness. The peace of the self comes from learning to live with holiness as we integrate the various parts of our self-our intellect, our will, our strengths and even our weaknesses-and direct them toward loving God in each moment and every circumstance.

*Lord, My Father,*
*Help me to be the best version of myself.*
*Give me strength when I am weary.*
*Give me patience when I am worn.*
*Give me courage when I am fearful.*

♦ ♦

*"Before I formed you in the womb I knew you, before you were born I dedicated you, a prophet to the nations I appointed you."*
Jeremiah 1:5

Knowing that we are created in the likeness and image of God and that we are created to do HIS will, we can begin to prayerfully discern His will for us in the everyday. Additionally, our service becomes a way of fulfilling our purpose rather than keeping us from our purposes. Once we have identified our gifts and how we can more fully use those, we will naturally be more intentional in our actions.

One obstacle to purposeful action can be our inability to recognize our real talents or gifts. It is often easier to recognize the skills of others than it is to see our own skills. We live in a world that requires our action or reaction, but not necessarily a deep understanding of our own gifts.

Other times, we may recognize our own gifts, but fail to value them. Valuing our gifts is different than recognizing our gifts. We can say, "sure I am gifted with special musical skills, or writing"… but if we don't value that gift, we are less likely to use it. Perhaps it wasn't valued when we were growing up, or maybe it is a part of us that we haven't fully embraced.

This is the difference between self-concept and self-esteem. I can have a healthy self-concept and understand my strengths in organization and communication, but if I do not value those skills, my self-esteem may be low. I may personally identify my gift to relate emotionally to others, but if someone I love deeply values logic and reasoning over emotional connection, I may start to doubt the importance of my gifts and skills.

It can be challenging to describe ourselves, but it is a good exercise in recognizing our unique set of gifts. Just trying to describe ourselves can be an insightful practice.

*When meeting new people, how do you introduce yourself for the first time?*

What you do every day is not WHO you are. Spend some time now in the quiet and ask God to show you who you are. Do not move on to the next section until you have answered these questions.

*God, what is unique about me? What are my gifts? How have I used those gifts during this past week?*

_____

_____

_____

_____

_____

_____

*Look at the gifts you listed and
circle those which you value in yourself.
Are these gifts something you value or do you find
yourself wishing you had someone else's gifts?*

INTEGRITY

*How do you give of yourself in a way that glorifies God?*

♦ ♦ ♦ ♦ ♦

*Lord, My Father,
You have created and designed me with intention. Grant me eyes to see myself anew. Help me to value all that I am, and all that You have created me to be.
Amen.*

## Challenges to Our Integrity

*"Watch carefully then how you live,
not as foolish persons but as wise,
making the most of the opportunity,
because the days are evil.
Therefore, do not continue in ignorance,
but try to understand what is the will of the Lord."*
Ephesians 5:15-17

Life gives us plenty of opportunity to have our character challenged, and so we must rely on the Holy Spirit to help us maintain our integrity. It is the Holy Spirit Himself who gives us the possibility to live a life of integrity, for it is the Holy Spirit who provides us with the gifts that enable us to practice virtue. For instance, the wisdom to know God's will and act with charity in specific situations, the counsel to respond prudently, and the fear of the Lord which helps us to practice temperance are just a few gifts poured out by the Holy Spirit.

We all have times where we recognize we are not acting like daughters of God. I admit there are times when I respond with irrational irritation to my children's little transgressions, or turn to distraction rather than engaging more purposefully with my family. There are nights when I fall into bed and realize I failed to give a bedtime blessing to one of my teens or a word of encouragement to a friend who is struggling. Most often these failures in integrity come when I am simply tired. My bedroom is on the second story just above our garage. When my teen comes home I can hear the garage door open, the slam of the car door, the closing of the garage door and then the slam of the door to the house. It is a four-stage call for me to get out of bed and check in with him.

But I don't always answer that call. Sometimes I nudge my sleeping husband and ask him if he wants to go say hi, and other times I give into exhaustion and simply pull the covers up a little more under my chin and drift to sleep with a guilty conscience. I know I should get up and go say hello, but I struggle to be consistent.

The tedium of daily life, interlaced with joy and stress and excitement and disappointment, lends itself to an inconsistency of character.

The little imperfections of humanity are just that—imperfections. As we practice our role as a good loving daughter, we must realize that *it is a practice*. We aren't perfect, which is why our lives must be lived in partnership with the Lord. We need constant support, direction, reinforcement, and even forgiveness from the Lord as we live day-to-day in His service. Remember that God's love does not require perfection from us. He wants us to grow in holiness and sacrifice, and at the same time He loves us perfectly in our current imperfections.

It is normal to strive for integration of character. When we evaluate and consider our own conceptions of who we are and our actual behaviors day-to-day, we must be forgiving of ourselves as the Lord is forgiving of us. A nightly examination of conscience and regularly going to receive absolution in the sacrament of Penance can help us to see places where we need to specifically invite the Lord in for deeper healing or help.

It is important not to dwell too deeply on those imperfections because doing so can lead some people to either despair or a rejection of the virtue they are striving to practice. When we are met with inconsistencies in our character or characteristics that fail to be integrated into our understanding, it is natural to first reject the inconsistency. Perhaps we make an excuse or justification for the mistake. There seems to come a point, however, when we are unable to live with the continual inconsistency, and that leads us to a rejection of the initially perceived or understood self-construct. Our minds cannot handle the cognitive dissonance.

Cognitive dissonance is a fancy psychological term that refers to the problem our brains have dealing with contradictory information. For instance, if you consider yourself to be a kind person, but you snap at a loved one and make them cry, you can excuse it as an isolated event. If, however, you consistently snap at people and cause others around you great distress, at some point, if you have any self-awareness at all, you may conclude that kindness is perhaps a characteristic that does not come naturally to you. You may decide that you are, in fact, more direct and honest than you are kind, and simply stop trying to cultivate that aspect of yourself.

This is gravely dangerous.

Rather than striving for holiness and recognizing the inconsistency in your character as a challenge which requires prayer and grace from the Lord to resolve—and which He is fully capable of doing—you choose to resolve your cognitive dissonance alone by changing your actual concept of yourself.

When you see inconsistencies in character, go to confession for your resolution; don't accept a less virtuous path where you attempt to resolve inconsistency of self by rejecting your integrity.

> *"Blessed is the man who perseveres in temptation, for when he has been proved he will receive the crown of life that he promised to those who love him."*
> James 1:12

The Lord doesn't require perfection from us. He does, however, desire that we use the gifts we are given in a way that brings Him delight. If you don't recognize your own skills and gifts, you won't be open to using them. Father Parks, the priest who called me out of my comfort zone to start the podcast, once said, "God gave me a gift and He DELIGHTS when I use it." He continued to explain that God doesn't need us; He is the creator of the universe, but we exist anyway. So the logical conclusion is that God must WANT us, each of us. He doesn't need you. He WANTS you. He wants you in this world.

To be living a life of integrity means to recognize your strengths and weaknesses as part of your being created intentionally by the Lord. Fully accepting who you are leads you to more confidently value your gifts and show consistency of character irrespective of the setting.

If you are a kind person, you are kind in all situations and you practice kindness because you value that trait. You are kind, not just when you are interacting with strangers, but also when you are tired or hungry or frustrated with others. Our nature is tested when we are tempted, not when we are comfortable. Living with integrity means you retain your character in the face of adversity, not just during the pleasant times of life.

◆ ◆ · · ◆

*Lord, My Father,
Pour Your grace upon me
that I may live with integrity
all of my days.
Amen.*

Chapter 3

# INTENTIONALITY

*"For as in one body we have many parts, and all the parts do not have the same function, so we, though many, are one body in Christ and individually parts of one another. Since we have gifts that differ according to the grace given to us, let us exercise them."*
Romans 12:4-6

In Chapter 12 of St. Paul's First Letter to the Romans, he explains how each of us has different spiritual gifts and are each a different part of the Church and Body of Christ. The chapter ends with saying, I shall show you a still more excellent way - LOVE. So taken together, LOVE is the way to stop comparing. We need to value our gifts and those of others and love them too as the body of Christ. There is such beauty in our diversity. No one is like you, so no one can give in the way you can give.

When we are content with the gifts that the Lord has given to us, and use them as only we can, we are fulfilling our purpose. When we can do so in a self-giving way like Mary, and really turn ourselves over to the service of the Lord through loving in action, this service actually becomes a way of validating and reinforcing *who* we are. We are living the life we are designed to live, in a way that uses our special genius, and it is aligned to God's will.

Can you describe one gift or talent or trait that you have that specifically helps you to <u>love</u> more fully?

_____

_____

_____

_____

◆· · ·◆

*I praise you,*
*because I am wonderfully made;*
*wonderful are your works!*
*My very self you know.*
Psalm 139:14

## Hypocrisy

None of us were raised by perfect parents.

As wonderful as many of our childhoods may have been, there probably came a time when you began to understand hypocrisy as a hallmark of adulthood. Hypocrisy is one of the big killers for families and relationships. At times we will fall short, and similarly people we love will fail to meet our own expectations. It is important that in these times of disappointment, we handle the disappointment with grace, and that we seek reconciliation with one another, and when necessary, with God as well.

God has already taken upon Himself the sins of the world—all those sins that have been and are yet to be committed.

We are a fallen people.

We are prone to mistakes, to responding rashly, and even to sin. But through the saving power of our Lord Jesus Christ and the sacrament of reconciliation, we can be made anew. We can be restored. When we fail, we need to apologize, we need to do penance and ask for the grace to be led away from that temptation in the future. And we need to be honest with ourselves. If we aren't honest about our struggles, how can we grow through and overcome them?

Previously I asked you to identify an area, situation, or time of day in which you find your consistency being challenged. I want you to think now about any relationships that prove to be a struggle for you in terms of integrity. Are there social situations or interpersonal interactions that frequently lead to you responding in a less virtuous way? Jot those down now and offer up a prayer inviting grace from the Holy Spirit the next time you encounter such a time.

♦ · · · ·♦

*Lord, My Father,*
*Free me from the need to be elevated by others,*
*from the temptation of perfection,*
*from the vice of hypocrisy.*
*Amen.*

## INTENTIONALITY

Too often we struggle against God's will for our life. Other times, we muddle through our journey completely disconnected from the reality that God has given us a specific mission to live out our lives in a particular way. That can lead to discontentment because our minds are occupied with that which is before us in the earthly realm while we remain disconnected from the interior life with Christ. We fail to recognize or use the specific gifts the Lord has given to us. We allow fear or failure, rejection or criticism to prevent us from stepping into that which we know God intends for us.

Sometimes we become so busy, we forget to be intentional, mindful, or purposeful. When the silence finally comes, our exhaustion takes over. Loneliness creeps in, and we look for something to distract us. I reach for my phone to click and scroll until I see something that fills me with worry, or dissatisfaction, or envy. Rather than filling the emptiness, it makes the emptiness even more apparent.

We are discontented. If we are going to grow in contentment, we have to grow in love. In order to grow in love, we have to strengthen and deepen our prayer life. True charity, true love is love for our neighbor *out of love of God*. Without an active prayer life, we will find ourselves going through the motions and failing to act in real charity towards our family.

Other times we begin this process of prayer and attempt to conform our will to His will but are left feeling inadequate or inauthentic. Although *imposter syndrome* is a real psychological construct, it can be used by the devil to keep us from striving to act in accordance with God's will for our lives. I want to encourage you to "fake it until you make it." Faking it is not wrong when we are acting in accordance with God's will.

Do I always *want* to read a book to my daughter? Nope. Or stay up a little later to spend some time with my husband? Nope. Or be available for my sons when they come home from soccer? Nope. But I do want them to know that I love them. And in order to convey that message, *sometimes I have to do things that I don't want to do.*

It is not hypocritical to do something that you do not want to do. Our hearts, our minds, and our bodies do not always agree on what we should do. When we have conflict, when we really don't want to act in the way our hearts are asking of us, we need to simply do what St. Teresa of Avila said:

*"Don't think too much and do whatever opens you up to love."*

Love should be guiding us. When we let our head do all the leading, we can easily fall into a pattern of justifying our less-than-loving behavior. When we let our bodies lead us, we can easily fall into sin because our bodies are weak. St. Paul spoke of this frequently in his letters (see Galatians 5:17, Romans 8:13).

It isn't the successes at the end that characterizes a good daughter, rather it is what inspires her life and her actions that give the measure of her character. After all, as suggested by Father Basil Maturin in his book, *Spiritual Guidelines for Souls Seeking God* (2016), "We judge one another not so much by what we are as by what we are becoming, trying to be."

## INTENTIONALITY

*Have you ever noticed that sometimes it is the things about ourselves that we dislike, which end up being the same characteristics we find difficult to tolerate in others? What qualities or traits in others do you find most bothersome? Do you have those same qualities yourself?*

*In what areas in your family life do you struggle to be authentic?*

It is easy to act with integrity when we aren't challenged because integrity refers to our ability to maintain consistency of character in the face of adversity.

*Where do you find your little crosses or challenges day-to-day? What are your consistent daily frustrations? What are the most challenging times for you during the day? When do you see consistency in character being challenged the most?*

_____

_____

_____

_____

Invite the Lord into those times before they occur during the day and ask Him to soften your heart.

One aspect of life that can challenge our integrity is when we struggle to stand firm to the commitments we make. We waffle on our follow through or answer quickly without fully processing the request. Countless times in the last twenty years I have regretted saying yes to something I should have turned down.

For instance, I remember a few years ago trudging through the riparian center nearby as I loosely followed a flock of preteen girls on a field trip. The surroundings were pretty enough, and I busied myself by taking some photos of the birds and pretty ponds. They had ducks which, as you know, I found delightful. But not even the ducks made the trip worthwhile.

My daughter was not happy that I was there as a chaperone. It was cold and I detest being cold. And then the zipper on my riding boot broke. So I hobbled through the field trip disconnected from my daughter and became irritated that I had given up my morning. I like the outdoors, but I definitely volunteered too quickly without really considering if it would be a good fit for our circumstances.

In my desire to show others that I was an "involved mom", I simply said yes before really thinking it through. In reality, my lack of prudence meant that another parent was denied the opportunity to chaperone. Since then, I like to think I have been much more sensible about saying yes!

When we are more careful about our commitments, and we don't rush to say yes or no, it helps us to stand firm. These commitments can be bigger, like the yes to lead an event or chaperone, or they can be smaller things like saying we can grab something at the store for a friend. Irrespective of whether they are big or little commitments, being thoughtful about them will help us to keep our integrity.

There are three very specific and practical things that can help us retain our integrity and save us from hypocrisy in most situations. First, we must guard our speech and listen more.

Too often we talk and talk, but fail to listen to what we really need to hear in order to honestly respond.

Secondly, we must let our yes mean yes and our no mean no. If we say yes, then we must follow through on it. If we say no, then we mustn't allow ourselves to be persuaded. Saying no but then being manipulated into a yes undermines the ability for people to trust us and sends the message that we don't mean what we say.

This assumes of course that we have intentionally committed, rather than responding rashly. So lastly, standing firm to our commitments requires that we are intentional about our actual commitments. This applies to commitments large and small.

Strive to safeguard your integrity as His daughter, aligning your will to His will in the big and little things alike. There is nothing too big or too small to bring to prayer. Many of us think of seeking God's will when we prayerfully discern life transitions or we meet a crossroad. This is very important to do; however, *God's will for our lives is not limited to the big decisions.* I believe His will for us is more often revealed in little day-to-day decisions. He cares less about what college we choose or which career path we take and more about how we react to the little frustrations or disappointments of our day. He cares less about which parish we join and more about the disposition of our hearts when we show up for Mass. He cares more about the character we show, the virtue we exercise, the vice we turn away from, than whether we studied to become a teacher or an accountant, or moved from one home to the next.

## INTENTIONALITY

It isn't the big decisions that define us; it is the little ones that reveal our character and either create stronger bonds of love, or slowly work to sever those bonds. Living a life of integrity created in the likeness and image of God is not something that happens by chance. It happens when you make a choice, a decision to continually choose God over self. It happens when you intentionally make a *fiat*, a decree, a declaration that you desire to be the daughter God designed you to be.

We will experience failure because we are limited in our abilities. We are works in progress. We are perfectly imperfect. We reveal our true selves in the challenging times. This means being a daughter with integrity, to act with dignity and purposeful holiness even when we are tired, or stressed, or angry. It means taking the difficulties we are met with in stride and not letting them overwhelm us.

In the next section, we will discuss how we can draw upon our role as God's beloved daughters when faced with various challenges.

◆ ◆

*Lord, My Father,
I know that You delight in me as Your beloved daughter. Just receive my love and let me be with You. Let me soak in every moment with You so that I can draw from that well which will never run dry.
Let me remain with You.
Amen.*

# SECTION 2
# CHALLENGES

"We can even boast of our afflictions, knowing that affliction produces endurance, and endurance, proven character, and proven character, hope, and hope does not disappoint, because the love of God has been poured out into our hearts through the holy Spirit that has been given to us."

Romans 5:3-5

When I was growing up, my father always had a fondness for the phrase, "It builds character." We heard these words when we struggled with a hiking pack that was too heavy for our frame, experienced a struggle in friendship, got lost exploring, nursed a broken heart, or found ourselves with an unfair and disproportionate load of the family chores.

As a child, my family and I spent a week each year beach camping at Lake Powell. My dad and grandfather had purchased a little outboard motor fishing boat and it ferried all 5 of us, with gear, through the beautiful canyons to our little camping spots. As each of us 3 children got bigger in size and appetite, it became harder to fit us, the provisions, and the gear in the boat.

By the time we hit adult size, we each were allotted one backpack for our personal items, and my parents had transitioned to bringing mostly dried food. To make things worse, we had a few meals which were typically all government issued MREs. My dad was a weekend warrior with the Army Reserves and when he wouldn't have time to eat during drill weekends, he would bring the rations home for family vacation. He would simply say that if it was good enough for the U. S. Military, it was good enough for us. If we didn't like the dehydrated chicken ala king, we were told it was "character building."

Growing up, my dad's outlook on challenges as opportunities for growth became my framework for looking at problems life placed in my path.

Challenges lead to growth of the self. The most intense growth occurs under pressure, when we are made to think and act in new ways. One of the clearest ways we can grow in the face of challenges is in our trust. We must recognize that God wants us to succeed in holiness and then trust that He will equip us for the struggles that come, regardless of how difficult the challenges may be (Maturin, 2016).

We need to develop a deeper trust in Him, in the reality that we are created for a purpose, and that He has given us all that we need for the work He has put before us. He has carried us through trials in the past, and although we may endure suffering, that suffering can bring us closer to Him. Our challenges can bring us closer to the Lord because they create the opportunity for us to grow in endurance and character which leads us to hope. And that hope becomes a trust in the Lord.

Some of our challenges are temporary, some are recurring, some are longer lasting. Some challenges are issues that we are able to fix with effort, and some are outside our control to change and require an internal change instead.

In the next section, we will look at challenges, the crosses we bear, the way we compare and make our crosses even greater, and then lastly, the solution to these which can be found in recognizing, developing, and maintaining a consistent relationship with the Lord.

◆ ◆ ◆

*Lord, My Father,*
*Help me to embrace the challenges You allow.*
*I love You above all and trust in Your plan.*
*Amen.*

Chapter 4

## CROSSES

*"He summoned the crowd with his disciples and said to them, whoever wishes to come after me must deny himself, take up his cross, and follow me. For whoever wishes to save his life will lose it, but whoever loses his life for my sake and that of the gospel will save it."*
Mark 8:34-35

I sat in the modest yet bookish feeling office of the parish priest. I say *the* parish priest rather than *my* parish priest because although I came to him in my suffering, I was not Catholic. I wasn't yet part of his flock. Yet he extended his counsel to me with love, and I felt the love of the Father.

In his little office filled with books and religious art, we discussed the reality that usually when suffering occurs, people want to know why. Their questions come as a partner to the grief in all circumstances: *Why did I lose the baby? Why did my husband leave? Why didn't the Lord heal her? Why would the Lord provide all these people for me to love and care for but not provide me with sufficient employment?*

And underscoring all of these questions is this primary set of questions: Why does our Loving Father tolerate suffering? If He loved us, why would He allow suffering to occur? And why does the suffering remain, not just in general, but specifically in these cases?

My encounter with the priest led me to a profound understanding that there is never a sufficient answer to those questions, but there is beauty in the suffering and there is healing in the cross.

Our crosses are not something we typically want to take up and bring with us on our life journey. Most of us are looking for the first place to ditch a heavy cross. Can we hide it in the mess of our lives? Leave it in that dark corner of our heart? Stuff it into the empty bottle at the bottom of the rubbish bin? We don't like our crosses. The last thing we want to do is hoist them on our shoulders and bring them with us each day.

In Mark 8:1, Jesus is clear. If we want to follow Him, we can not leave that cross behind us. He goes on to explain that we also have to be willing to give up our very lives. We know that Jesus was likely foreshadowing the death of the apostles here, but for the rest of us in modern times, we too must be willing to give up our lives. We must be willing to walk away from our very lives, our hopes, dreams, plans, and accept a new life with Him. We must be willing to surrender our temporal wishes and pursue a life with Him as His beloved daughter, accepting our crosses as they come.

## CROSSES

*What larger crosses do you bear? Sometimes we push these larger crosses aside so as to focus on the positive. That can be a great coping mechanism, but can also prevent us from really surrendering our problems to the Lord.*

_____

_____

_____

*Sometimes our interactions with people can be a sort of cross. Who are the individuals that most challenge you?*

_____

_____

_____

◆◆◆◆◆

*Lord, My Father,
I long to see the beauty in this cross.
Give me the trust to embrace the cross and bind myself ever closer to You in my pain.
Amen.*

## Emotionality

Too often our emotional response to a situation can become the actual cross, rather than the event that produces the emotion. The reality of a sick loved one, for instance, can produce fear, anxiety, despair, and even a lack of hope. These emotions then become the cross we are unable to manage.

When we are suffering, the temptation is to dwell in misery. Every effort must therefore be made to release oneself from the present pain, injustice, malice, anger, and rather to allow God's love to permeate. We must learn to stop ruminating on the specifics of our own cross.

Crosses don't have a solution that can be solved if one just spends more time or attention on formulating an escape plan. When we face challenges, there is rarely a sufficient answer for the question we love to ask: "Why is this happening?" Suffering happens regularly and mysteriously. And yet we search for the answer in the hope that it will somehow make sense of the inexplicable.

This is intensified if the challenge is wrapped in some injustice. As C.S. Lewis (1976) noted, "Men are not angered by mere misfortune, but by misfortune conceived as injury. And the sense of injury depends on the feeling that a legitimate claim has been denied." Injustice makes it harder to accept suffering and entitlement leads us to interpret suffering as unjust.

If Our Lord chose to suffer and die for us, and we hope to live in His image, won't we too be asked to suffer? If Christ did not escape His cross, what makes us think we should escape our own? The crosses we bear are part of our process, part of our journey, part of our path.

This does not mean however that we need to let our crosses define us. They are a part of us, but they are not who we are. We are daughters of God and defined by that alone. We are also widows, grieving parents, recovering alcoholics, single mothers, cancer survivors, war veterans. These other aspects of our life are part of the whole of who we are, but they do not define us.

Our crosses, big and small, are our path to holiness.

Embracing those crosses in the midst of the problem is very difficult to do. It can help, however, if we recognize the relationship between patience, obedience, and charity. It is out of love for the Lord that we are obedient to Him, and we show that obedience by acting with virtue regardless of the stresses of this earthly life. Our crosses can help us to grow in virtue and grow into a deeper, more trusting relationship with the Lord.

## Embrace Your Cross

In order to do this, we must change our mindset to enable us to embrace the crosses of everyday life as part of our personal journey as His daughter, not just to muddle through. When you are faced with challenges, keep two things in mind to help you to navigate the difficulty with greater confidence: First, remember past times when God was abundant in His mercy and grace. Next, recognize that we all will face difficulty, and it is this difficulty that gives us the opportunity to show our true nature.

When the pleasantries are stripped aside, when trials face us, our core character is challenged and we have an opportunity to show God and man that we want to be His daughters.

Our everyday choices give us the opportunity to grow in holiness and grow deeper in relationship with Him. One of the primary ways we can do this is by treating those around us as the Lord wants us to treat them. They are His beloved, just as we are His beloved. Who are those individuals that most challenge you? Ask the Lord to help you to love them in the same way that He loves them.

We are asked to stay constant to our relationship with God through the challenges. Responding in anger to the Lord is understandable because He has the power to relieve us of the suffering, but God Himself is not the one inflicting suffering upon us. In our fallen world suffering should be expected and God should not be the one to receive our anger or frustration when suffering is experienced. Rather, we should stay constant in our love for Him, even when it is hard.

Turning away from the Lord is a temptation for a suffering soul, but doing so only brings further pain. Our Loving Father is alway there to welcome us back, no matter how long we have been away.

*Take a minute to think back upon this past week. When did you find yourself struggling? Did you try to draw closer to God at that moment? If you have not yet taken that moment to prayer, do so now. Simply tell God how you felt. Were you hungry, angry, lonely, or tired at that moment?*

---
---
---
---

*List one source of stress you currently face, and reframe that situation in the positive. It can be an immediate, short term stressor or a chronic stressor.*

---
---
---
---
---

*Lord, My Father,
I turn this frustration over to You.
I ask that You help me to love through the difficulty.
Amen.*

◆ ◆ ◆ ◆

Developmental psychologists describe cognitive growth as a process by which the brain is stressed and stretched, and growth results as an outcome of this pressure. Brains which are not challenged do not face the same level of growth.

Athletes know this to be true of the body as well. In order to get a muscle to grow and become stronger, the muscle fibers themselves must be shredded through exercise. They must undergo pressure in order to grow stronger; this growth is uncomfortable and even painful at times. I recently came across some research on what is called *athlete's heart*. Cardiologists report that some endurance athletes have a heart with greater mass, different heart sounds, and even some restructuring of the actual organ. The intense training leads to a changed heart.

So too of our spiritual life. We have to look at the painful challenges as opportunities to grow. We must undergo stress in order to grow in virtue. In the book of James, we see a beautiful perspective on suffering. The letter instructs the readers to not only endure, but also to face the trials with pure joy:

> *"Consider it all joy, my brothers, when you encounter various trials, for you know that the testing of your faith produces perseverance. And let perseverance be perfect, so that you may be perfect and complete, lacking in nothing. But if any of you lacks wisdom, he should ask God who gives to all generously, and ungrudgingly, and he will be given it."*
> James 1:2-5

Even if we think that suffering may serve a purpose, it is hard to understand why we should face it with joy. But St. James explains that when we encounter suffering, we have the opportunity to exercise our faith. It is in the midst of struggle that we really are able to show the areas in which we are strong and those in which we are weak.

Trials have a way of getting our attention. True, suffering can draw us closer and deeper to Him. However, it can also turn us inward and fill us with despair. How can we embrace our suffering rather than let it overwhelm us?

In order to use suffering as a way of growing in holiness, we have to work to change our emotional state of mind. If we can not change the actual situation, we need to change our reaction to the situation. We need to accept and welcome suffering as a way of growing.

Father Thomas Dubay (1989) writes, "There is a close correlation between suffering well and growth in prayer depth. Of itself, of course, suffering improves no one, for a person can become bitter in his woes. But trials borne with love and in union with the crucified Beloved make one grow by leaps and bounds."

*It's time for an easy question now:
How do you react to stressful situations?
How does that change depending on the situation?*

_____

_____

*Create a practical plan for responding to one source of chronic stress in your day. Draw upon your personal strengths. God has prepared you for any suffering he will allow.*

_____

_____

Father Mark-Mary Ames, C.F.R. suggests in his 2021 book, *Habits for Holiness*, that we strive to develop the habit of uniting sacrifice with prayer. Little sacrifices made in prayer or larger suffering done with intention can alike be used for spiritual good. He writes, "the greatest force in history is prayer united with sacrifice." Many of us make regular sacrifices but do so without much intentionality. Uniting those little sufferings with prayer can be a first step towards developing a great spiritual practice.

This practice can also help us to embrace rather than avoid suffering at all costs. When we have an "avoid at all costs" attitude towards suffering in life, it is easy to justify the avoidance of uncomfortable things that are actually the morally correct thing to do. Making the right choice can bring personal suffering. If we can approach the situation with great love and prayer and sacrifice, suffering can be endured for great spiritual benefit. When we approach suffering as a thing to avoid at all costs, sometimes that cost is our actual spiritual self.

## Solution through Service

*"Amen, I say to you, whatever you did for one of these least brothers of mine, you did for me."*
Matthew 25:40

Many of us in helping professions or in the midst of family life are called to serve His children every day. Serving others should not be a distraction from our spiritual life, but rather a way for us to grow in holiness through loving service. When we consider our role as teacher or mother or friend as an avenue for us to serve God, it has the potential to change our entire outlook. We quite literally are living for those who are in our midst, because we love our Father in heaven.

For instance, many friendships are tested in adulthood as we move from intense friendships forged in high school or college to friendships of convenience. We meet people at work or through our children's activities, and these are the most easily created friendships. But navigating which of these relationships to cultivate into a deeper friendship can be trying, and at times the relationships to which we find ourselves bound to can be very difficult. If we adopt an attitude that we only have friendships to fill our needs, then we will undoubtedly be disappointed. If we enter into friendship with the awareness that we are in relationship with others to serve God, not the other or ourself, that can help.

As we grow into adulthood, many of us also find that our relationships with family members become difficult in a different way than in childhood. We are adults and crave adult interactions, yet it is easy to fall back into childhood roles when we are around members of our family of origin. Even in these frustrating times, we still are called to serve our Lord with love. The Lord does not become any less deserving of our love or attention just because we are annoyed by our family. When we treat others with kindness, we serve the Lord.

> *"Our sanctification does not depend as much on changing our activities as it does on doing them for God rather than for ourselves."* Lawrence, 1982

We need to see the beautiful opportunity we have to serve the Lord by serving our family and friends as a gift. Some individuals are invited into a life as a missionary, and will travel to far off places, visit convicts in prisons, and take vows of poverty, chastity, and obedience as a way to serve the Lord. But even if we are not a religious sister or typical missionary, we are a missionary in our own life serving Him from the comfort of our homes, or dorms, or offices. Dressed in our pajamas and slippers with cold coffee in our mugs, or sitting at a desk, or driving our carpool, this is our missionary field.

I knew I wanted to be a stay-at-home mom even before I was married. Although I also desired a professional life, giving up the time at home with my young children was unthinkable. Each of my child development classes seemed to reinforce the idea that this was right for me–which was important because my decision was not well received by everyone. I remember a friend saying that if his daughter went through four years of college and seven years of graduate school like I did, only to be a stay-at-home mom, he would expect her to pay him back for the wasted expense. This attitude is shared by others too, I know. My husband overheard a co-worker refer to a stay-at-home professional wife as a "Paycheck-Sitting-At-Home." Too often, value is found only in the financial gains a person can provide.

My confidence that staying home with my children was the right thing for me probably came from my own mother. She was a nurse in a hospital prior to becoming a mom, and she returned to nursing as a school nurse when we were old enough to be at home for a few hours alone. When she was home with us full time she served us with all of her heart. And when she returned to nursing she found a new way to serve the Lord with love. Whatever vocation you are being called to serve, embrace the chance you have to serve the Lord your God with all your heart and mind and strength.

Did you know that serving others is well-known as an antidote for depression? Being a psychologist by training, I have theorized two possibilities for this correlation. First, when we act in an altruistic fashion we actually like ourselves better. We feel better about ourselves because we are doing good to one another. Willing the good of another is one definition of love. When we serve others with a pure heart, we are acting out of love, and loving altruistically can heal our hearts.

Additionally, when we serve others in need, it helps us to grow in our awareness, gratitude, and appreciation for our own life circumstances. It helps us to be more aware of what we have to share, our wealth both literally and figuratively. Gratitude is a precursor for joy. We cannot experience real joy without first having a thankful heart.

*In what way could you share your gifts more generously with others? Write out a concrete plan including a timeline for completion of this service.*

_____

_____

_____

_____

*Lord, My Father,*
*Thank you for the people in my life.*
*Thank you for endowing me with gifts to share.*
*Give me strength and humility as I serve You by serving others.*
*Amen.*

Chapter 5

## COMPARISON

*"Are you envious because I am generous?"*
Matthew 20:15

In *The Way of Perfection*, St. Teresa of Avila outlines three important things for the spiritual life. People who do these are able to advance in the Lord's service, and, without them, you cannot hope to become a great contemplative. First, St. Teresa says one must have a love for each other. This must be the perfect love. It is a love of the virtues and the inner goodness in each of us that comes from God. Next, we must have a detachment from all created things. Lastly, we must have true humility. This is the most important as it embraces all the rest.

As I reviewed these three things, I realized that having a spirit of comparison or competitiveness is the antithesis of these three things. If I am judging others with a prideful heart, I am not seeking humility. If I am jealous of the earthly life, comforts, or love that others have, I am not detaching myself from this created life. If I want to be elevated or blessed above someone else, then I am not showing love for that person.

We live in a world that feeds on a competitive spirit and leaves us hungry, but comparison and the jealousy it brings are as old as humanity. We read about the brotherly strife between Cain and Abel in the biblical book of Genesis. God favored Abel's sacrifice over that of Cain, and Cain reacted by killing his brother Abel. Comparison is a natural way of evaluating the world around us and helping us to find our proper place, but when that comparison leaves us unhappy, it opens the door to sin.

Is there someone in your life whom you are jealous or envious of because of some aspect of their life? I recently realized I was jealous of a dear friend's spiritual life because of the way she describes the Lord using images in their prayer time conversation. It was so silly to be jealous of that, but it is natural to be jealous when others are experiencing things that you also desire. The awareness of it is necessary in order for you to protect against the spirit of envy. *Of whom or of what are you jealous?*

---

*"Christ made my soul beautiful with
the jewels of grace and virtue. I belong
to Him whom the angels serve."*
St. Agnes of Rome

When we grow jealous of the gifts of others, we fail to trust that the Lord has provided us uniquely with that which we each need to grow as His daughter. We have been given everything we need to succeed at the specific task that the Lord has laid out before us. That is what we were created for–with intentionality and divine wisdom. We were not designed to do another's work, and thus we are not endowed with their gifts. Envying the worldly achievements, the size and shape and nature of another's life will strip away the joy from your life. Selfishness, envy and pride get in the way of true happiness which can only be obtained from a relationship united with your heavenly Father. *It is through Him you will find the joy you so desperately seek.*

I encourage you to not concern yourself with that which does not concern you. Use *your* talents and skills. Don't envy others, don't compare, don't judge. Honor their skills, honor your own and you honor God. Don't get sidetracked by the circus around you! Don't allow envy to steal your joy or distract you from the pursuits God has placed on your heart. Your talents and gifts are possible because of the Holy Spirit working through you. Use those talents for His will in His kingdom on earth. Accept the gifts from the Lord and use them joyfully with gratitude.

> *"The spirit that he has made to dwell*
> *in us tends toward jealousy...*
> *God resists the proud, but gives*
> *grace to the humble."*
> James 4:5-6

*Lord, My Father,*
*Let me remain forever*
*in Your loving arms.*
*Help me to be humble.*
*Amen.*

## High Standards

Growing up I had a best friend who was like a sister. She stayed the night during the school week, went on family vacations with us, and had her own seat at our dinner table. But when we went to high school, something happened. Without any words, we suddenly had a falling out. I wondered for years what happened and only as an adult did I discover that my high standards for myself and for her were simply something she was tired of trying to achieve. The pivotal moment in the demise of our friendship came one weekend when I was singing my first solo in church. I had been in the choir for years, but this was my first ever full solo. I had practiced for months and thought I needed my best friend in the front pew. Just a few days prior however she received an invitation from her dad to come visit. My self-focused teenage heart was hurt that she chose to visit her father rather than support me and so I sent her a nice guilt trip to take along with her for the weekend. As we entered high school we made different choices regarding boys and dating and how we spent our free time. My criticism and judgemental ways led to a lack of openness and eventually we simply drifted apart.

    I thought it was fine to have high standards and expectations for others as long as you had similarly high expectations for yourself. I had set the bar high for everyone and as such was frequently disappointed, not just by others but in myself too. Rather than accepting flaws as part of our nature, I saw them as a weakness. I strove for an unattainable perfection, and it damaged myself and my relationships as a result. Father Jacques Philippe explains that when we are more accepting of ourselves and our own flaws, we are more readily able to accept other people's flaws as well (Philippe, 2020). Oh how I wish I had become familiar with his works as a young adult!

## Know Thyself

> *"There are many gifts that we may envy in others, yet if we had them, they would be only a hindrance; If they were necessary for us, God would have given them to us."*
> Maturin, 2016

    Sometimes the most harm comes not in comparing ourselves to others, but in comparing ourselves to an idealized and unachievable standard which we have set for ourselves or accepted from our childhood. As mentioned earlier though, perfection is a rejection of our complete person. No amount of hard work or determination will allow us to achieve perfection.

Our idealized self is a fantasy that prevents us from truly knowing ourselves. By knowing and accepting both our strengths and our flaws we can come to find true humility. Growth in humility is an essential step towards developing a deep prayer life (St. Teresa of Avila, 2005).

Sometimes in our envy, we fail to see that others are successful because they have a particular talent or gift or characteristic that we do not have.

*What is one area that is holding you back? Are you socially uncomfortable? Do you have less organization or energy than you think you should? Are you quick to judge or anger? Where would you like to grow?*

_____

_____

_____

It can be humbling to honestly catalog our failures or faults, but doing so can help us to more deeply understand our gifts because our strengths and weaknesses are often woven together tightly. For instance, people who feel deeply and perhaps wish they were less emotional are also the ones frequently who are more emotionally aware of others suffering. What we see as a vice in ourselves, with perseverance and prayer, can become a

## COMPARISON

virtue with God's grace. Left alone however it can fester in the darkness and cause pain to ourselves and others.

*Look at your previous answer. How can you use that fault, area of growth, or aspect of your personality for the glory of God?*

_____

_____

_____

Let's take this same idea into a different context. Maybe there there tasks or responsibilities that you do not like to do and they may be holding you back from your best version of yourself. For instance, we may hate doing laundry and our dread of that task keeps us from being as organized as we would like to be. Sometimes when we have to do things we don't like to do, we fight it rather than surrender.

*What are you fighting that you should surrender?*

_____

_____

_____

Enough of the negative. Knowing thyself is about both understanding the positive and negative in our daily life.

*What is life giving you? What puts you in a great mood?*

_____

_____

_____

_____

## Process focused

Although we should strive to be our best, when we focus on the achievement, rather than on the process we will be disappointed. Being process-oriented rather than outcome-oriented is actually a predictor of overall well-being. We should be striving for holiness and wholeness, not perfection in the moment.

The self-giving nature consistent with our roles as women in this life leaves many of us to give until we feel as though we have nothing left. At times, we can't see any purpose to our lives beyond the keeping and caring of loved ones, and our purpose seems to be linked to our relationship with others. But our purpose comes from *Whose we are*, not some daily report card of how well we did according to, or in comparison with others.

## COMPARISON

It is easy to think that we are not doing things well enough when we compare our lives to that which we see of another's life. When we talk about spiritual life and our progress on the path towards fully receiving our inheritance as God's beloved daughter, we need to remind ourselves that our goal is not perfection, but rather holiness.

Striving for holiness will help us to love rather than resent the other who has gifts we wish we had.

Striving for holiness will help us to accept our challenges as the areas of growth rather than areas of failure.

Striving for holiness will help us to see those around us as individuals who can help us develop a deeper sense of self.

Two people cannot compete in terms of their relationship with the Lord. Do you envy the holiness of another? Comparison can only be good when it helps us realize how we too can grow. Think of someone who exemplifies a life of holiness and how you may be able to express that in your own personal way. I suggest that you pause just for a minute now and consider how imitation of this holiness can be a way of practicing spiritual growth.

We all will come to grow in relationship with the Lord in a unique way, but He is the same Lord, and therefore there often are similarities in how we can attain a deeper relationship. This is why emulating the practices of those who are further along their spiritual journey can be a good thing. But this is very different from coveting the life of another. Take that to the Lord in prayer before moving on.

◆ ◆

*Lord, My Father,*
*Please provide me with models of holiness that*
*I can emulate to help me grow through the*
*challenges I face. Help me to recognize my unique*
*gifts and keep holiness as my goal.*
*Amen.*

Chapter 6

♦ ♦ ♦

# CONSISTENCY

Remaining consistent in our role as God's beloved daughters can be a challenge for all of us. Particular challenges of character or situation tempt us to give up hope and give into despair. Challenges can easily draw us off our path and lead us to be emotionally responsive to our Father, rather than consistent in our relationship with Him. At times I know I have become angry or impatient with Him, rather than adopting humility and listening, or looking for ways He is asking me to grow. Maintaining consistency in our devotion to Him and showing perseverance in prayer irrespective of your emotional state is essential to growing deeper in intimacy with our Father.

In C.S.Lewis's classic *The Screwtape Letters* (1976) the antagonist presents us with the Law of Undulation, suggesting that humans are by nature inconsistent:

"While their spirit can be directed to an eternal object, their bodies, passions, and imaginations are in continual change, for to be in time means to change. Their nearest approach to constancy, therefore, is undulation – the repeated return to a level from which they repeatedly fall back, a series of troughs and peaks."

This undulation in behavior, thoughts, or general character is presented as fertile ground for sin as it keeps our minds focused more on the temporal experiences than the spiritual. We focus on how we feel rather than on who we love and turn our focus inward rather than upward. Developing and sustaining a routine for our prayer life is the antidote for the weakness of inconsistency.

## Practice of Prayer

Everyone, regardless of their station or vocation, can develop a routine for prayer. The second Teresian principle for spiritual growth based on the thoughts and writings of St. Teresa of Jesus, mystic and doctor of the Church, is that opportunities for growth in the spiritual life are not context or situation dependent (Dubay 1989). Opportunities are everywhere and found in every time of life. Prayer is not about spending hours dwelling on the complexities of the mind or the struggles of the heart. It should be about cultivating the ability to open the soul to God. It is about being humble in our invitation to God.

Some become too scrupulous about prayer and feel that if they can not commit, for instance, to a full rosary, then they should not begin one. The Lord rewards even our smallest efforts at connection with Him. You do not need a home altar and the right candles. You do not need a nanny to watch your kids or a full hour so that you can complete a holy hour each week. You simply need to *show up consistently day after day* according to a routine that works for you. He will show up–in fact, He's already waiting. The key is to maintain consistency even in our imperfections.

## Good Times

Some of us are good at prayer and attention to our spiritual life when things are particularly bad or particularly good, but struggle to remain consistent to the Lord when life is just fine. Maybe we will keep up our mass attendance, for example, but it becomes more of a show of attendance than an intention to fully participate in the Sacrifice of the Mass.

But here's the truth: God is in the little things, not just in the big things. Hurt feelings, feelings of inadequacy, lost car keys, late to appointments–don't wait for the big things to ask Him for help. Nothing is too big or too little for the Lord. It isn't just when children get sick that they need our prayers. Turning to the Lord is a practice, a habit to cultivate in the day-to-day.

We have to build into our days the habit of turning to Him and listening for Him. When we begin to notice Him in our day to day, it makes it easier for us to move forward in relationship with Him. What you do outside of formal prayer will help prepare you for your time in intentional prayer. One can't expect the mind to naturally become quiet in prayer, for instance, if it is never quiet during the day.

Different seasons of life will offer us different opportunities for quiet in our day. We cannot expect the same routine or discipline in each season. But what we can strive for is to build in some time or intentionality each day. We can be flexible but remain loyal. We can offer some prayers each day when we tidy up the toys or take the kids to the park. We can turn off the music in the car on our drive to work. I have a friend who says her rosary each morning when she showers before work because as a mom with a career and four little kids that is her only quiet time. If we're not intentional about cultivating a little time for prayer each day, it is easy for our relationship to fade. It's not because the Lord isn't there, but rather because we stop looking for Him.

When I was in graduate school, shortly before having children, my husband and I met a wonderful couple. They were smart, fun, and outgoing. The husbands had met in their MBA program and found that they were alumni from the same college on the East Coast. The guys formed a solid starter relationship in the school time and soon wanted the wives to meet. We met for dinner and admitted after the first hour that we both had a case of the nerves because our husbands wanted so much for us to get along–and we did! What followed were BBQs and basketball games; we both had labradors so we even did doggie playdates.

And then family life slowly took over. We had children at different ages with different interests. Demands of busy schedules left little free time for us to just hangout. Those evenings with long dinners or the late afternoon ball games became impossible to fit in. And we lost touch. There was no big fight or embarrassing faux paux. We just put other things first. We couldn't, or chose not to, invest in the relationship any more. Thinking about that now makes me really sad, because I love this couple. But our friendship just slipped away by accident.

Is this familiar? Perhaps you have friends with whom you chat infrequently. Without regular interaction and effort, a relationship cannot flourish. Think about past relationships you have had with someone you enjoyed, but with whom you have fallen out of touch.

*What are the lost relationships in your past?*

_____

_____

_____

_____

The same thing can happen with our relationship with the Lord. We sort of let things slip away because we make little choices each day to do something other than pray, to take the less virtuous road, to ignore His little tugging at our hearts. When we say yes to the Lord in the little things, it makes it easier to say yes to Him in the big things. In this way, we are able to develop a consistency of character. We develop a habit of behavior and a pattern of the soul.

Mikhail Gorbachev, the former leader of the USSR, said in a 2007 speech given at Harvard University, "If you aren't moving forward, you are moving backwards." He was referring particularly to the fall of communism and the opening of the East to Western ideas, but it could also be said about spiritual life. If we are not moving forward, it means our attention and energy is being diverted from the Lord, to the more temporal things of this earth. Spiritually we are moving backwards.

All that is required for spiritual growth is effort and trust. We must trust in the Lord that if we consistently show up, fully present to Him, He will be there. Sometimes we will hear Him clearly and sometimes we will not. But trust and faith give us the strength to return to Him even when we don't see or feel tangible progress. We are dealing with heavenly progress which is very different.

## Hard Times

*"I command you: be strong and steadfast!*
*Do not fear nor be dismayed, for the Lord,*
*your God, is with you wherever you go."*
Joshua 1:9

Sometimes, when we are experiencing great suffering or disappointment over unanswered prayers, we can find it hard to accept scripture such as this. But we can be assured that He is here in the big things and the little things, the good times and the bad times. When we experience trials, we also experience God's faithfulness through and to the end. His love for us does not depend on us, it is given freely.

The Lord doesn't require our praise in exchange for His love. He knows our hearts. He understands the heartbreak we feel, and His heart is breaking with us. But He wants to bring good out of even the most horrible situations. He hasn't disappeared; He will bring good from the pain. We need to consistently turn our struggles to Him. Just as the Lord never leaves us, we too should strive to be in constant relationship with Him even in our suffering.

We can become so consumed with aspects of our life that aren't in our control. We question the Lord's role, His love, His very presence. It is in these times we need to turn away from the problem and seek the Lord.

When one of my children was in the neonatal unit I was wrecked with exhaustion and fear. Leaving a baby at the hospital is one of the hardest things I have had to do in my life. I had older children to care for and was healing from my third c-section, but all I wanted to do was sit at her bedside. In my physical and emotional stress I reached out to friends and family and asked them to lift me up in prayer. I asked them to pray the words that I was too weary to pray. I knew I needed the Lord and I felt his presence with me, but I just didn't have the words.

We are not alone in our struggles, nor will we be overcome by them. When the burden gets too heavy sister, turn that over to the Lord in surrender, and open yourself to His love. When we take His yoke upon us, we are tied to Him. Only through surrendering our struggles to Him can we maintain that consistency through the challenges.

*Are you closest to the Lord in the good times, the bad times, or the little every day times? Think of a major life event you have experienced, good or bad, that you can remember vividly. Where was God in the midst of that experience?*

_____

_____

_____

_____

By continuing to turn to Him with consistency, we both acknowledge and invite His constant presence. We need to continually be inviting Him in, and when we do so we are best able to see that He is present.

> "Do not fear: I am with you; do not be anxious:
> I am your God. I will strengthen you, I will help you,
> I will uphold you with my victorious right hand."
> Isaiah 41:10

As humans, it is normal to struggle in a relationship. It is okay to get angry with the Lord and to tell Him how you feel. There is a story in the Carmeliate oral tradition in which St. Teresa of Avila exclaimed, "Oh my Lord, when wilt Thou cease from scattering obstacles in our path?" To which she heard the reply, "Do not complain, daughter, for it is ever thus that I treat My friends." The quippy St. Teresa is said to have replied, "Ah, Lord, it is also on that account Thou has so few!"

If we can maintain consistency in our prayer life, it can help us to not be swayed by emotion. Rather, we simply spend a time each day turning our hearts over to Him, when we are happy or sad or angry or disappointed. We never want to let our emotions separate us from Him.

When we can turn to, rather than away from, our relationship with the Lord in times of struggle, we deepen our relationship instead of making it more shallow. We need to be honest with the Lord. He can handle our anger, our frustration, our sadness, and even our doubt. You need to just keep talking to Him. Keep showing up for the conversation even when you don't have anything to say. He is here with us even when we don't want Him.

When we are suffering the temptation is to dwell in misery, or to ruminate, mumble, blame, and complain. The solution is to invite God into the present moment of suffering, and allow God's love and light to permeate. We need to surrender our sorrow to the Lord.

This means we must stop ruminating on the specifics of the cross (Philippe, 2020). Crosses don't have a solution that can be solved if one just spends more time or attention on formulating a plan. When we can't change the situation, we must change our response to the situation. Our aim should be focused on turning our minds upward and outward rather than inward.

*Think of a time in your life when you were angry with the Lord. How long did that last and how did it get resolved?*

_____

_____

_____

_____

Maybe you are still angry with God. Sometimes in the deepest grief we can lose even the desire to reconcile with the Lord because we still hurt. If you weren't able to resolve the pain and anger you felt, tell Him now how you feel and invite Him to heal your hurting heart. At the very least, ask your heavenly Father to help you gain the desire to reconcile with Him.

"Is anyone among you suffering? He should pray."
James 5:13

One of the primary tools we have for showing more consistency in challenging times is to be mindful of God's will for all of our lives as His daughters. In its very first paragraph, *The Catechism of the Catholic Church* states that we were created to love, know, and serve God. Therefore, we live out our purpose in the little ways we serve God, in the little things we do that show love to God and neighbor, and in the time we devote to better know Him.

## CONSISTENCY

When we draw nearer to God, we allow ourselves to experience a greater depth of emotion and experience an emptying of the self before the Lord. When we empty ourselves emotionally in prayer, we give the Lord the chance to fill us. In this way, we need to attempt to cultivate the process of entering more fully into the suffering, so that we can be redeemed by the love of God.

In the next section, we explore real, practical, and important ways that we can develop our own practice of prayer and grow in our ability to better surrender to Him every day. The Lord is with us always, and we should strive to be consistent as well. It is only through prayer that we will come to a deep understanding of who we are to Him, and what He wants for our lives.

◆✦✦✦✦◆

*Lord, My Father,*
*You know me and love me in my strengths*
*and my weaknesses. Let me grow in my ability*
*to turn to you with confidence when I struggle.*
*Help me find my strength in Your love.*
*Let me leave my burdens at Your feet as*
*I enter Your loving embrace.*
*Amen.*

## SECTION 3
# PRAYER

> "With all prayer and supplication, pray at every opportunity in the Spirit."

Ephesians 6:18

"A piece of the couch."

Such was my friend's answer to the question, "Where do you find peace?" It wasn't even the whole couch. All she got was a *piece* of the couch. But it was her place. Where she could find peace in her home. It was her happy place.

One of my grandmothers had a little table in the kitchen. It was scarcely large enough to fit her bible, journal, and coffee cup. But it was her space.

My other grandmother had her "nest." It was her special comfy chair in the corner. It had a resting place for her crossword books, nail file, and a coaster for her nightly martini.

All three of these women found a resting place in their home. A place for meditation, contemplation, relaxation. Some of us have a special place, but others find their peace among the pots and the pans. They meditate on the rosary while they drive to work or walk on the treadmill. They converse with the Lord while they wash the dishes. They listen to the whisperings of the heart while they nurse the baby.

For many of us, normal life is physically and emotionally demanding. Both physical and emotional exhaustion infringe on our ability to really foster a healthy prayer life. When we make prayer a priority, act in a purposeful way to cultivate a prayer life, and build prayer into our daily life and personal culture, we are able to not only cope through the stress, fatigue and fear, but we are able to grow in love and holiness.

Finding time to pray in the chaos is an essential step to growing in the spiritual life.

One of our goals should be to fuse our inner life with the outward life–that is, to learn to pray at all times and prioritize our relationship with the Lord. As Father Jacque Philippe reminds us, "Prayer is a school, an exercise in when we understand, practice, and deepen certain attitudes toward God, ourselves, and other people–attitudes that gradually become fundamental to our whole way of being and acting" (Philippe, 2008). I aspire to this–most days feel like I am still in the elementary grades of this school.

I am learning though that I need not detach from my duties, but rather bring God into those duties and relationships. St. Teresa of Calcutta said, "You can pray while you work. Work doesn't stop prayer and prayer doesn't stop work. It requires only that small raising of the mind to Him: I love you God, I trust in You, I believe in you, I need you. Small things like that. They are wonderful prayers" (St. Teresa, 2006). This is not to say that we shouldn't also strive for times of quiet prayer. For when we allow ourselves to enter into prayer deeply, our lives outside of active prayer will also be transformed.

Dubay (1989) writes in his book *Fire Within* that, "lifestyle and prayer grow or diminish together. If people today or in any age lack mystical prayer, it is not because it has been tried and found lacking. It is the Gospel that has not been tried." He explains that if you want your prayer life to improve, you need to fix your life and be intentional about living with virtue. Rather than seeking solutions to our problems in prayer, we should look at the life we are living, the choices we are making, and consecrate every action to the Lord. Only then can we hope to be able to live in prayerful unity with the Lord as His precious daughters.

Perhaps it can be described with the psychological term *intersubjectivity*. When people are around each other often, maybe as roommates or siblings or spouses, they develop a sort of shared understanding of circumstances. Wouldn't it be amazing to have that sort of connection with the Lord–to be able to love others the way He loves, and see situations the way He sees them? I know I would love to be able to hear His voice and feel His guidance all the time.

Children and parents alike have an uncanny talent at being able to hear one another's voice in a crowd. This comes not from a biological process, but from their constant communication. It's the same with our relationship with God. Drawing near to Him each day in prayer helps you to attune yourself to God's will so that you can confidently say yes to the demands of His love.

As His daughter, you need to be able to hear His voice irrespective of the situation. In this last section on prayer, we will begin to evaluate the way we have structured our lives and identify changes we can make to cultivate our ability to hear and respond to our Father's voice in the crowd.

This is an active process. Call on Him. Invite Him in. We are created for a relationship with the Lord, and He is a kind and good and loving Father. He pursues His beloved daughters and invites us into a deeper relationship with Him. He doesn't force it. He awaits it.

*"The Lord is near to all who call on him,
to all who call upon him in truth."*
Psalm 145:18-19

Chapter 7

## PRIORITIES

*"For where your treasure is,
there also will your heart be."*
Matthew 6:21

I remember a few years ago, looking at the people going into daily mass as I dropped off my kids at school. I thought "someday that will be me."

Someday I would be the one going in there because I would have more time.

Someday I would go to adoration or benediction.

Someday I would pray a daily rosary.

Years before that, when my first three were even younger, someone suggested that I carve out an hour each day for prayer. *Really?* I thought, *I can't even use the restroom in privacy.* But that conversation gave me a goal: to make prayer life my priority.

In reality though things didn't quite work out right away.

When my last little one started preschool five mornings a week, I started working a few hours a week for a women's ministry, and then it was more. Just when I had reached the point in my life where previously I had said, "Then I will be better about prayer," I found something else important to do.

It was good and holy and valuable work to do and I don't regret it, but the reality was I wasn't making my own life with Christ my priority. When I had a few minutes, I would check my email, I would get caught up in other stuff because there is always something else to do. Once again, I was putting off making my relationship with God the most important in my life.

In the same way that we are able to show consistency of character in the big and little choices we make, we also have an opportunity to grow closer or to distance ourselves from God as a result of the big and little choices we make. We prioritize whether to let Him into our space or not. We choose to distract ourselves or to grow quiet. We choose to continue to embrace the chaos or to master it.

> *"The man can neither make, nor retain, one moment of time; it all comes to him by pure gift."* Lewis, 1976

How we spend our time reflects not just who we are, but *Whose we are.* If we are a people of prayer, we must learn to prioritize prayer. Jesus said it best: "seek first the kingdom [of God] and his righteousness, and all these things will be given you besides" (Matthew 6:33). We generally find time to return text messages, to exercise, to check social media, to turn on a show or play a game–but do we make prayer a priority?

*"Time is not the real problem. The real problem is knowing what really matters in life."* Philippe, 2008

Do you move from being busy to being distracted? We are often almost frantic in our work, but then the moment we have free time, we seek distraction. Social media scrolling, TV show binging, social media stalking… none of it feeds us. It simply sucks away our time. We escape from ourselves, from our thoughts and fears and anxieties, rather than more fully examining our hearts.

God wants us to renounce those things that separate us from *Him*. Maybe it is that show He wants you to renounce so that you can go for a walk with your spouse or have a cup of coffee with a friend, or play a hand of UNO with the kids, or take a few extra minutes for prayer time and journaling with Him. Maybe He wants you to renounce that glass of wine that makes you just mellow enough or not really want to talk to anyone or engage in the evening routines of the household. Maybe He wants you to renounce your self-righteous indignation that leads you to believe your spouse is incapable, or your intellectual arrogance that pits you against loved ones in conversation.

We all have our own vices that keep us from greater intimacy with God. I admit, I love my word games, my historical fiction, my evening glass of wine, and although none of these are in themselves sinful, they can be a distraction that keeps me from conversing with the Lord. They are things that I turn to when I want to fill the silence rather than retreating deeper into the silence where I will hear Him.

*Father,*
*You are the source of all wisdom.*
*Help me to be wise to the things in my life that separate me from you or distract me from doing your will every day. Give me the eyes to see with clarity what needs to be removed so that I can grow closer to you.*
*Amen.*

♦· · ·♦

I know, life is hard and often overwhelming, and it is so easy to try to escape. But the Lord wants you to bring it all to Him.

Lent is the traditional time to look at our lives and examine those things that separate us from greater intimacy with the Lord. Some of us, let's face it, attempt a life-makeover. In a surge of inspiration, we purge our closets and eat healthier and maybe we instill some greater discipline in our prayer life. But all too often we forget that we are all unique. We adopt some fun way of focusing on God or minimalism during Lent rather than actually finding a way to enter into a deeper relationship with Him–which is the point. *The purpose of the fasting and abstinence is intimacy*, but this often gets lost or forgotten as the weeks advance. And then we enter into Easter or Ordinary Time and forget that we should continue to grow in relationship with God.

I recently let my time on our parish school's advisory board expire. It had been a good experience and a place where I could use my gifts. However, at this time it isn't uniquely situated for me. I discerned that I need to be available at night to my family. It was hard to say no because it is a prominent position and it looks good on paper. I admit, it fed my vanity. But my decision wasn't made alone–I brought it before the Lord in my prayer time and slowly He revealed His will. You, too, will have opportunities to use your gifts–often very good opportunities–that may not be His will. How do you discern? Prayer can help reveal those areas in your life, those vices, or commitments that need to be pruned away so that new growth can occur.

Sometimes we might feel that we are not positioned for a deep and meaningful relationship with the Lord because of our life circumstances. Sometimes life feels too full for a deeper encounter. God rewards our generosity of time and our giving nature both, but I ask you if you are serving God through your business, or if you are serving to feed your pride and self-worth. They are not the same thing. Our lives are fulfilled by the Lord and should never be too full for Him.

Sometimes what we are asked to give up is not inherently bad. As women, we sometimes warp the natural generosity of our hearts and start giving to fill our pride. We like the recognition and gratitude of others–that's natural; all women have a desire to be seen. But ultimately that kind of self-giving leaves us feeling unfulfilled because we were giving for the wrong reasons.

If you are a giver, as all women are, look at the areas where you are giving and pray about those. Are you giving according to your gifts and out of love for God, or are you giving so that you can feel accomplished?

When we are able to detach from the things that fail to bring us closer to God, and enter into the pursuit of virtue instead, we are rightly ordering our lives. In doing this, we free up space and energy for a continual pursuit of the Lord. We clear away the temporal distractions and free up time and energy for prayer.

If our actions are going to reflect our lives, we have to be more careful about what we do. We have to set limits for ourselves and know when to say no. Think for a minute about your own life. What is God asking you to renounce? What is keeping you from greater intimacy with the Lord? What do you turn to instead of opening the word or delving into prayer?

He won't ask you to renounce your gifts, and He will not call you to do something oppositional or threatening to your vocation. In *Divine Intimacy,* Father Gabriel writes, "anything contrary to obedience and our duties cannot be inspired by Him" (Gabriel, 1996).

## PRIORITIES

*What in your life separates you from God, your loving Father? Is it a favorite activity, a nasty habit, a lack of self-control? Is it the busyness that you create in your life? Is it a less-than-healthy relationship?*

---

---

---

Who knows us better than the Lord? No one. Not your earthy parents, not your coworkers, not your best friend, boyfriend or spouse. Yet we often let our relationship with these people define who we are, rather than finding our identity in relationship with Christ. As daughters of God, we are meant to be imitators of Christ. Being true to ourselves therefore means living a life of integrity by living out who we are as precious, unrepeatable daughters of God.

We have to know what to say no to, but we also have to know what to say yes to as well. Focusing on saying yes to virtue rather than no to vice is called *positive holiness*. It is a concept I first discovered reading Father Basil W. Maturin's work. I mentioned Father Maturin previously, but if you will indulge me to share a little more about his life it may be instructive. Father Maturin was an Anglican priest who became a Catholic priest at age 51 and served as chaplain at Oxford. He was a priest, preacher and writer.

In 1915, Father Maturin perished along with 1,194 other passengers aboard the RMS Lusitania when it was struck by a German U-boat. In the last moments of his life, Father Maturin was seen to be giving last rites and helping others into the lifeboats. His love for man was greater than his fear of suffering. His devotion to the Lord, greater than his desire for self-preservation. I share this bit about his life and death because the reports of his death show that growing in holiness can be as simple as making the hard but simple choice to choose virtue in the face of a challenge.

His concept of *positive holiness* is all about growing in love rather than mastering sin. As we grow in love, it should help us to push away sin. This approach can be a great tool for those of you who generally stay away from traditional vice, but want to grow in holiness.

Maturin describes the difference as he presents the Ten Commandments versus the Beatitudes. The Ten Commandments provides predominantly a list of vices that we should strive to avoid. Keeping the Sabbath holy and honoring thy Mother and Father are the only two of the ten that are stated in the positive. Contrast this to the Beatitudes that list eight dispositions of the soul to which we can all strive towards.

I have a pretty easy time avoiding the sins outlined in the Ten Commandments. Using those as a guideline sets the bar fairly low for my personal behavior and it is an easier achievement. When I look at the Beatitudes, I see a list of virtues that I can continually strive towards.

We have so many no's inside of us. It is a wonderful thing to be able to examine our life and ask ourselves—to what can we say yes?

## The Beatitudes

*"Blessed are the poor in spirit,*
*for theirs is the kingdom of heaven.*
*Blessed are they who mourn,*
*for they will be comforted.*
*Blessed are the meek,*
*for they will inherit the land.*
*Blessed are they who hunger and thirst for righteousness,*
*for they will be satisfied.*
*Blessed are the merciful,*
*for they will be shown mercy.*
*Blessed are the clean of heart,*
*for they will see God.*
*Blessed are the peacemakers,*
*for they will be called children of God.*
*Blessed are they who are persecuted for the sake of righteousness,*
*for theirs is the kingdom of heaven."*
*Matthew 5:3-10*

*What is it that God is asking from you today? Read through the Beatitudes again. To what virtue can you say yes? Is He asking you to be more present and loving, to step out of your comfort zone, to suffer, or maybe to trust Him with something? Take a minute to think about this.*

_____

_____

_____

_____

Father Gabriel of St. Mary Magdalene, O.C.D., a Discalced Caremelite and author of *Divine Intimacy* (1996), takes this concept one step further by arguing that ultimately we should focus less on virtue itself, and more on simply loving the Lord and growing in relationship with him: "Rather than aim directly at correcting a fault or acquiring a virtue, it would be much more profitable for us to maintain a continual dependence on the Interior Teacher, and to act only after listening to His intimate, sweet voice." This is a shift then from doing the right things to please God, toward loving God so intimately that you act in such a way as to constantly remain close to him.

## PRIORITIES

*What steps can you take this week to begin to meet the specific call and grow in love and relationship?*

_____

_____

_____

_____

◆ ◆ ◆ ◆ ◆

*Loving Father,
I desire to grow. I long to be more like you and your saints. With your grace I can both grow in virtue and find the strength to turn from vice. Let your grace flow over my heart and mind that I may better know you, love you, and serve you.
Amen.*

When my kids were really little, I found it very hard to progress through my normal to-do list most days due to the constant interruptions or the endless demands of the children. The longer the list, the harder it actually seemed to accomplish ANYTHING. And if I was stressed about a deadline–forget it.

It was in the midst of one of the frustrating mornings a dozen years ago that I discovered one of the paradoxes of parenting: the more I pulled away from my children, the more relentless they were in their demands. However, when I frontloaded my morning with attention, and patience, and snuggles, and care … and when I loaded them up with one-on-one interaction really smothering them … the more peaceful the home became, the more ordered the rest of the day could be, and the more opportunity I had for my own tasks.

My children are all in school now leaving me with a to-do list that looks fairly similar, and I have the opportunity to generally work uninterrupted, but I have found that the paradox still applies–*to my spiritual life.*

When I set aside my lists and my panic about deadlines or too much to do in so few hours, and I just rest in prayer, I am rewarded tenfold. When I make time to be one-on-one with my Lord, and let My Father smother me with His love and peace, I am able to proceed with peace and prudence and a great wisdom of what does and does not need to be a priority for that specific week or day or even hour.

I used to think that if I just had more time and less of everything else, I would be better at prayer. I was wrong. Time wasn't the issue.

This became even more clear when I had a series of surgeries that each had me laid up for a few weeks. I was so confident that while in bed recovering, or waiting for surgery, I was going to be able to have some awesome prayer time. I bought spiritual books, I set aside an area to keep them within reach, I had my nicest pens and journals handy. I was set.

And my prayer life didn't change one bit. It is embarrassing to say, but I just binged watched a show and snuggled with my little girls. It made me realize that the lack of a prayer life was because I had my priorities disordered, not because I was too busy.

God doesn't demand much from us. We can pray while we work, while we drive, while we cook, while we clean, while we take the kids for a walk–whenever. He is everywhere at all times and doesn't require an appointment (although scheduling time with Him can help immensely!). But our Father doesn't care if we are dressed or are late or even if we have brushed our teeth or put on clean clothes. He just wants us to show up.

I hope you aren't beating yourself up at this point for not being in constant prayer! This is something we'll both be working on our whole life. But think back to the gospels. In the first chapter of Mark, Jesus got up early and went out to a deserted place and prayed. Simon came and found him and said, "Everyone is looking for you." You see, even Jesus carved out quiet time for prayer. He, God Made Flesh, Son of God, made prayer a priority in His day. We can again look at scripture when we want to see how God wants us to order our lives.

*"As they continued their journey He entered a village where a woman whose name was Martha welcomed him. She had a sister named Mary [who] sat beside the Lord at His feet listening to him speak. Martha, burdened with much serving, came to Him and said, 'Lord, do you not care that my sister has left me by myself to do the serving? Tell her to help me.' The Lord said to her in reply, 'Martha, Martha, you are anxious and worried about many things. There is need of only one thing. Mary has chosen the better part and it will not be taken from her.'"* Luke 10:38-42

Read the scripture again and try to picture yourself as either Mary or Martha. Now read it a third time and picture yourself as the other sister.

*Which came more naturally? With which sister do you more closely identify? I think I am a natural Martha who is striving to live more like Mary.*

# PRIORITIES

The problem with Martha is that she was distracted by the work and unable to see what the Lord desired of her in that moment. She came to the Lord asking Him to fix her sister, rather than asking, "what do you desire of *me* right now Lord."

For many of us, the problem with our prayer life and the shallowness of our relationship with the Lord is not because of time or work load. It is because we are unintentionally (or sometimes intentionally), allowing ourselves to become distracted. I am my own worst distraction. St. Augustine's famous line could have been written for me when he says, "You have made us for yourself, O Lord and our heart is restless until it rests in you" (St. Augustine, 1961). I struggle with both a restless heart and a distracted mind. Instead of taking time to sit in silence or close our eyes and pray, many of us fill the emptiness with meaningless distraction, which only leads to a deep loneliness.

Distraction is one of the most subtle and effective tools of the devil because it often feeds our pride, yet leads to a deeper loneliness. We feel important when we are busy, and we feel noble when we serve to the point of exhaustion. Distraction keeps us from focusing not only and most importantly on the Lord, but also from focusing on those people around us who need, who crave, our love and attention.

I want you to all take a minute and list your greatest distractions. Maybe it is your to-do list. Maybe it is the care of an older loved one or your own little ones. What is currently preventing you from taking five minutes to rest in the Lord? You have to identify your distractions before you can move to solutions. You have to recognize your individual problem before you can solve this problem.

*My Greatest Distractions to Prayer:*

1. _____

2. _____

3. _____

4. _____

5. _____

Truth be told, my biggest distractions are my own pride and social media. It is pride that prevents me from letting go of the fact that the floor is covered in dog hair, or that the laundry needs to be done. The sin of pride tells me to put my to-do list above time with the Lord. It tells me I need to look accomplished to others. It tells me I am failing if the house is a mess at the end of the day or when we run out of milk.

And then there is social media. When I have five or ten minutes waiting to pick up kids, or—in my previous life—when the baby went down for a nap, or when I found myself needing to just tune out the world, it was social media that distracted me from using that special time to be with the Lord. Rather than just listening to His voice in the quiet, or saying a decade of the rosary, or offering up my frustrations or suffering of the day for a friend, I would tune out the thoughts and scroll.

But when we use our precious free moments for the Lord, we show Him that He is our priority. And more and more, our lives become rightly ordered with God at the center. We recenter ourselves rightly before the Lord.

The reality is, we all have an endless list of things that need to be accomplished each day. Often it seems as though I take my task list for the week, and just duplicate it for the next week. We have specialty tasks–make that doctor appointment, turn in that paperwork, get the oil changed, and then we have all of those repeating, background tasks–groceries, meal prep, pick up kids, drop off kids, sweep the floor, wipe the tables, take out the trash, wash the clothes, fold the clothes, dress the kids, undress the kids, wash more clothes . . . it's just the stuff of life. Putting off any of those things for fifteen minutes generally won't hurt. If the dinner is fifteen minutes late, if the grocery run is delayed, if you get the oil changed tomorrow instead of today… the world won't stop turning.

The problem is the list seems so big, so long, that we can't set aside fifteen minutes for prayer until that other stuff is done. *But sister, it is never done.* That is one of the truths of being a woman. There is always something else to do. As soon as you think you are done you are going to get hit with, "Can I have help with this project due tomorrow" or "We are out of bread" or someone will come home with a fever, or a referral for glasses, or a note that your skills and talents are needed somewhere immediately. Trust me, I understand. But I know that God wants more for you.

I chose that scripture of Mary and Martha precisely because it is such a tough one for women to accept, mainly because it is still today so applicable and most of us can identify with Martha. I have Jesus waiting before me, and I busy myself with other work and then feel resentment because I didn't give Him my time or attention.

*Do you have unrealistic expectations of what your life, your work, your home should be and look like? Where do your expectations of your life come from?*

Who sets your priorities?

## PRIORITIES

*To which tasks have you intentionally chosen to say "yes" or "no"?*

---

---

---

*Are the demands you place on yourself external or internal?*

---

---

---

*Are there things in your day-to-day or weekly routine you can delegate to others or reconfigure so that they are less demanding of your time?*

---

---

---

Our priority should be to strive to remain in the Lord's company as we serve Him while serving others. If you are looking for gratitude or praise from your others, you will be disappointed because they can never give you the satisfaction equivalent to the sacrifices you are making for them. Your satisfaction with your vocation has to come from the confidence in your heart that you served the Lord as His faithful and trusting daughter.

I was in prayer recently and I felt unsettled by my to-do list. It is hard to calm the buzzing in my head sometimes, especially when the list is long, so I asked the Lord to order my day. I asked Him to make it clear what was and was not a priority. I left the adoration chapel, got back into my car, and picked up my phone. There was a text from my infant niece with her photo and the caption from her mother's message was, "Will you come snuggle me?"

I sat in the car, looked at my list, looked up to the Lord and said "Really?"

And then I drove directly to my niece's house. We spent some time together with her mom and I left their home with the greatest sense of peace. We have to abandon our priorities and ask the Lord what *His priority* is for our day.

Would it be hard for you to ask the Lord to order your day? Are you able and willing to surrender that sort of control to the Lord? Are you ready and able to practice abandonment? It is hard! But if we can begin to let Him order our day, it becomes easier to let Him order our life.

## PRIORITIES

If we can't surrender the little things, how can we possibly be expected to surrender the big things? Letting the Lord order our life begins with prayer. Pray before you sit down to do your schedule or list making. When you are met with a decision, ask the Lord to help guide you.

Father Jacques Philippe writes about the attitude of detachment in his book on spiritual peace (1991). He says that when we adopt an attitude of detachment we are often not asked to give up everything. However, it is the surrender and the *willingness* to give it all up that bring peace.

He writes, "The proper attitude then is simply to be disposed to give everything to God, without panic, and allow Him to do things His way, in total confidence." God ultimately knows what is best for us because He knows us better than anyone. He knows us better than we know ourselves because He alone designed us.

To surrender is to give all completely. To surrender means to give up care for, care of, and responsibility for a solution. It becomes the Lord's problem, not yours. The Lord may use you as an instrument of His will, but only with your permission.

Too often we give God a conditional surrender. We file a complaint and ask for help, we communicate our worry or concern, but we do not quite give it all over to Him with complete abandon. We share the burden, make requests, and then keep that concern carefully tucked in the dark corner of our heart. Real surrender means giving it all over without explanation, without constraint, without restrictions.

*What burdens your heart right now? Do you really want to surrender it or do <u>you</u> want to solve it with God's help? Do you want to be the hero?*

_____

_____

_____

_____

Trust in the Lord to heal the hurt or worry and turn it all over to Him.

We were created to know, love and serve God–so ultimately what we do every day should be ordered according to whether it helps us to know, love, and serve Him. As daughters, we get so caught up in serving others that we don't give ourselves the opportunity to know Him or show Him love. And we can't really be serving Him if we don't know what His will is for our life. Prayer is the answer. It helps us to surrender the frustrations in life, informs our decisions, provides us with peace, and informs our practices so that we can be women who act purposefully and who live a life of integrity.

*Lord, My Father,*
*There are times, Lord, when I feel so weary. I grow tired of feeling inadequate. I am tired of feeling like a failure. There is never enough time or money or energy to satisfy everyone. Help me to realize that I am trying to satisfy others in a worldly way, instead of striving to serve you in holiness. Help me to strive instead to satisfy your most sacred heart. Help me to measure myself by your most holy standards. Remove from me the desires for temporary rewards and place in me the longing to meet your desires each day.*
*Amen.*

Chapter 8

◆ ⋅ ⋅ ⋅ ◆

## PURPOSEFUL

In order to make prayer a priority in our busy life, we have to make a purposeful decision to surrender to Him, to trust in Him, to allow Him to reward our trust with grace. And while it is harder to do this when we are pulled in a million different directions, we can still cultivate a prayer life.

You have to be purposeful and practical about developing your prayer life just as you are purposeful in how you spend your money, how you choose your friends and carve out special time to spend with them, how you spend your free time. Consider how everything important you do is done with purpose and thought. If I don't set aside special time for date nights with my husband, those date nights are very unlikely to happen. If you don't set out a special time with the Lord each day, you cannot expect to have it.

We can purposefully develop prayer in our lives in three ways. First, by making time with God part of the rhythm of our day. Next, we can work towards developing a contemplative heart and bringing Him with us throughout our day. Lastly, by cultivating and recognizing beauty around us, we can grow to recognize Him in the everyday. These habits are important to develop because most of us live a life filled with distraction.

We can't escape the craziness of life. We have to find silence in the chaos. We have to look beyond the husband or roommate on a call in the other room, the piles of dishes and laundry, work deadlines and demands of family, and seek His face in all of it. Because if we don't, we will fall into loneliness and despair, becoming bitter and resentful. We will see our situation and relationships as obstacles to our spiritual growth, rather than recognizing that our relationship with the Lord, and our ability to love Him by loving others, is our precise path to holiness.

> *"Our actions should unite us with God when we are involved in our daily activities, just as our prayers unite us with Him in our quiet devotions."* Lawrence, 1982

Unless we are purposeful in aligning our actions as service to the Lord, the actions are depleting, and we grow weary. If we really want to be more holy, we need to simply act as a disciple and serve the Lord as a loving daughter. We need to get out of our own head, stop complicating it, and act. We need to become childlike in our dependence and obedience.

Our time is not our own. It is the Lord's to do with as He pleases. What pleases the Lord? How often have you asked yourself or Him this question? I encourage you to shift your attention away from simply what pleases you, towards what pleases the Lord. This does not mean we can not and should not ever have time for leisure or for rest and true recreation. Sometimes that is precisely what the Lord wants for us, and we need it on a regular basis. But our goal should be to embrace our personal time because it pleases the Lord, not because we strive to become inwardly focused and self-indulgent.

◆ ◆

*Good and Loving Father,
Thank you for the joy you bring into my life.
Help me to better interpret the times when
I need leisure or recreation versus
when I should rest with you in prayer.*

St. Paul tells us to pray without ceasing (1 Thessalonians 5:17). But the Greek word in this passage, *adialeiptos,* doesn't mean non-stop, it means *reoccurring*. When we are interrupted by life we need to accept, embrace, and then return to prayer. In his wisdom, St. Paul knew that earthly life gets in the way of our eternal life.

Life is loud and busy and chaotic—all the more reason to set aside intentional prayer time. The busier we are, the more diligent and disciplined we must be about making the time for a relationship with the Lord. We must be specific and set the time. I really encourage you, as challenging as it is, to keep that time for your spiritual growth.

## Order

When I was in college, I asked my mom how it was that she and my dad were always so good at working out and staying fit. She said that she scheduled it and didn't give herself the opportunity to back out. If she was supposed to work out, she never thought, *Should I work out today?* She made the decision based on logic before the time came and didn't give herself a chance to overthink it. It didn't matter if she felt like it or not. It was good for her so she was going to do it.

Our prayer life has to be like that too. Yes, prayer time can be awesome. But it can also be dry sometimes. And *we still need to do it*. We are to "persevere in prayer" (Colossians 4:2). What sorts of things do we have to persevere in? We persevere in the tough stuff. He doesn't say "indulge yourself in prayer." Prayer can be hard. Be logical, be thoughtful, schedule it, and just do it. Never ask yourself "Do I feel like praying right now?" Or "Should I pray now or later?" Just do it.

When we make prayer our priority by ordering it into the routine, we actively set aside our will and surrender to the will of God. When we abandon our own desires and fears and concerns and sit in the presence of the Lord, we are rewarded with inner peace.

Developing a ritual of prayer is the first step. The ritual of prayer helps us to develop a pattern which becomes a habit, and this habit helps us maintain the proper inner disposition even when we are not in active prayer. If we show up only when we feel like it we are relying on our emotions to guide us rather than our faith or devotion to the Lord.

I know that I don't always feel like praying, and sometimes I don't even think of it. All too infrequently when faced with stress my limbic system kicks in and I move into Flight-or-Fight mode (usually, for me, it is fight-stance!). I don't automatically move into prayer-stance. But the more committed I am to my routine of prayer, the easier and more natural it is to adopt prayer mode when life stresses hit.

What is the first step to developing a ritual? How do we begin to enter into prayer and fit one more thing into our day?

We can turn to scripture for a little help. In the Gospel according to Mark, we read that Jesus woke up early to pray. "In the morning, rising up a great while before the day, he went out and departed into a solitary place, and there he prayed." Jesus too was constantly surrounded. So He got up early to pray. Jesus woke up early anyway, even when His human body may have been tired.

Ordering our day with prayer time set aside daily, purposefully, is the first step to really developing a stronger prayer life. It cannot stop here, however. If our prayer life simply becomes part of the routine, it can become an obligation rather than a freedom. Once we are able to cultivate a habit of prayer, we need to cultivate a more contemplative mind. For in this contemplation, we are able to meet God the person throughout the day and come to know Him intimately. He begins to inform our patterns and direct our responses.

He walks the journey with us, hour by hour.

## Contemplation

*"It is necessary to leave our interior turmoil in order to find God. Despite the agitations, the busyness, the easy pleasures, God remains silently present."*
Sarah, 2016

We live crazy, busy lives. Learning to slow down and intentionally separate oneself from the craziness is counter-cultural. Some families really rely on two incomes. Other women are on their own and work tirelessly to put the food on the table and keep a roof over their head. Even in these situations, though, I encourage you to do everything you can to cultivate times of contemplation into your every day. This will come easier for some of us than others!

Sometimes I think that if I had converted to Catholicism as a teen, I may have become a contemplative religious sister! I love the quiet. I love my prayer time. I love thinking, reading and writing. I love the schedule and routine found in praying every few hours. I have a contemplative calling.

When I first converted, I gave a lot of thought to my vocation as a mother. I came to believe, incorrectly, that contemplative life is not compatible with motherhood. In reality, contemplation can be found within any vocation. We are all meant to respond, react, think of others and their needs, wants, and desires. We are asked to be self-sacrificing and self-giving. It is not dependent on age, or stage, or station in life.

Developing a contemplative life within any vocation means making time for prayer daily, being intentional about setting aside time and not being discouraged when your vocation pulls you away from your conversation with the Lord. Cardinal Sarah (2016) says, "The Father waits for his children in their own hearts." God isn't a genie who poofs away when someone else enters the room! He is always there.

As our life unfolds and changes, so too should our prayer life. Prayer life will look differently at different stages in life. For most of my life, prayer consisted of an Our Father before bed. I remember visiting my grandmother when I was in jr. high and she came into my room to tuck me in and pray with me. I didn't know how to pray. Her Southern Baptist heart was more than mildly disturbed and I no doubt became the object of many of her prayers in the years to come. But she sat with me and each night that week we prayed the Our Father together.

The habit of nightly prayer stuck with me as I grew into adulthood. When my children were young, we prayed family prayers before bed, and as I have grown in my love of the Lord, I have added my own private prayer time. Gradually as my relationship has grown stronger, I added a holy hour each week before the Blessed Sacrament, daily mass, spiritual direction, and about an hour of daily morning prayer. Little by little the Lord has called me to more–more time, greater intimacy, and deeper devotion to Him.

When I think back on my early years of parenting in particular, I wish I had devoted more time to prayer, but it was something that didn't develop overnight. I have built it up over the years just a little at a time. That said, we can always work toward a deeper relationship, regardless of our stage in life.

Whatever our life looks like, greater intimacy with Him will always benefit that life. I encourage you to do the hard thing and build a new habit of prayer into your day because the reality is we can all accept the Lord's invitation into a more contemplative relationship with Him.

A contemplative life must be built on the foundation of daily mental prayer. We all need the peace and strength and guidance that comes from this kind of prayer, which is described as quiet personal prayer. I am talking about prayer that includes a vulnerable sharing of one's self, but also silence in order to hear the Lord and be receptive to His love and guidance. In fact, frequently there is much more silence than anything else. In conversation, silence is the invitation for another to speak. Silence brings with it a disposition of listening so that there can be a dialogue rather than a monologue. It is in this listening that the relationship grows.

We need one-on-one interaction with the Lord in prayer, and the grace that comes from it in order to prepare us for the struggles of life. Believe me when I say this: Prayer in the good times acts as a sort of protection for the tough times. The Lord we grow to know and love certainly won't abandon us when we find our lives in turmoil.

*Jesus speaks that there is only one thing we need (Luke 10:42). What is the One Thing you need? What is He speaking into your heart and offering you?*

---

---

---

---

*What One Thing can you turn over to Him this week? What One Thing can you entrust completely to Him? Maybe you aren't an anxious person, but do you have an ever present or recurrent concern that gnaws away at you?*

---

---

---

---

Lord, My Father,
I am your daughter by design. Awaken within me my purpose and supply me with grace, that my day may be ordered. Remain present in my heart and mind. Amidst the tasks and struggles of daily life, keep my heart closely aligned to your will.
Amen.

Chapter 9

## PRACTICAL

*"How can anyone teach another the form of
conversation with a friend?
It grows, unfolds, develops of itself."*
Maturin, 2016

Sometimes when a muscle or joint is super tight, a therapist, rather than stretching the area, will compress it in order to get it to relax. It seems counter-intuitive, but it works to help that area to relax. And sometimes, it is the same in our spiritual lives.

One night I found myself in one of those parenting moments of heightened anxiety. Maybe it was the storm outside, or the cancellation of practices (I am horrible with changes to the schedule), maybe it was the soundtrack of our life with the thump - thump - thump of the soccer ball against the wall and the chatter of the girls interrupted by thunder outside. I found myself in the kitchen barely keeping it together. I took deep breaths and tried to show prudence in my response to the little loves and their requests, all the while feeling a constriction in my entire torso. It was at that moment that I just gave in. I gave into the tightness and stress and confusion in the schedule. Rather than continuing to stretch myself, I constricted. I turned inward–or rather upward. I grabbed my rosary and went room to room asking each of the kids at home if they wanted to join me for the rosary. *Right then.* In the dining room. I sat with my teenage son, and we just prayed. And as promised, peace came over us and over the home. We went from physical division in our home with people in different activities and spaces competing for attention, to unity in the name of Jesus.

Four things in this situation were bold and new for me.

1. I prayed in a very public space.
2. I invited the kids to join me instead of demanding it or hiding from them.
3. I added something sacred during a time of day when I typically was simply responding to the needs of others.
4. I put order to the chaos rather than becoming overwhelmed.

Let me be transparent and tell you that in moments of intense frustration, I rarely have the wisdom to turn to prayer. But just as it is counter-intuitive to compress a muscle that needs to be stretched, when we are stretched beyond what we think we can tolerate, we too must compress, and rest in the Lord.

And sometimes that means adding something to an already full or overwhelming situation. Rather than stripping away tasks on the list, sometimes we need to add prayer to the top.

Since that day I have spent other days in prayer while my children were around. Sometimes they join me, most often they do not. But in making my prayer life a priority, they are witnessing a proper ordering of my life. They have also seen that praying the rosary is something tangible, and possible, and something that they too can choose.

But more often, I spend time in prayer away from them. When my little ones are around, I feel constantly pulled from one request to another. And for me, bringing the Lord with me through the day has to start with private prayer, and it has to incorporate quiet time in my day for mental prayer and reflection. Without my private prayer ritual, I don't have the base to pull from to remain in the presence of the Lord in the day to day.

## Praying When You Don't Feel Like It

*"If you have lost the taste for prayer, you will regain the desire for it by returning humbly to its practice."*
Blessed Paul VI, 1971

Praying is not always easy. If we can maintain a ritual, it will help move us through the times when our prayers are dry, or the voice of the Lord is silent. Just as our prayer life will change us, it too will change dynamically as we grow. At times we will want to pray, and at times we just want to distract ourselves from what we are feeling or experiencing. I encourage you to take that to God too. He created us and is appreciative of the complexities of our hearts.

Over the course of our lives we will experience loss, anger, frustration, betrayal. We will be angry and sometimes this anger will be directed at the Lord. Regardless, I encourage you to still show up to prayer. Maintain the ritual. Share with the Lord your heart. He can handle it. St. Teresa of Avila said, "The sole aim of beginning to practice prayer should be to ENDURE TRIALS, and to resolve and strive to the utmost of her power to conform her own will to the will of God." The goal of prayer is not to relieve us of any problems, but rather to help us to endure those trials and help conform our will to the will of God. How can we possibly know the will of God if we don't pray?

Our prayer time is going to be reflective of our schedule and the demands on us, just as all our time is influenced by life events. Prayer is the easiest thing to cut from the day when the hours tick at rapid rate. Yet I encourage you to maintain that ritual, through sick kids and long work hours and summer vacations and Christmas parties. Don't let the very thing that will sustain you in your struggles, be the thing you cut from your list. Find a way to continue to come to Him in prayer, even when you don't feel like doing so. Make adjustments, but keep some semblance of ritual. Trust me, I know this from experience!

I recently found myself at the end of a tough series of weeks. The kids had returned to school after a long Christmas break, but then illness and injury had someone home fairly consistently. I found my prayer routine disrupted, my daily mass attendance spotty, and my time for quiet reflection or journaling scant. I was starting to become unsettled by the slightest frustration, and I was overreacting to everything and everyone. Weeks before, I had committed to attend a worship night at a nearby parish. I couldn't back out because I didn't have the phone number of the woman I was supposed to meet. I felt trapped by the commitment, but begrudgingly decided to go.

An hour later, I knelt before the Blessed Sacrament, with my forehead on the cold floor, and my shoulders shaking, as tears streamed off my face and onto my sweater. In this room filled with women, praying, singing, and giving honor to Him, I was able to finally release everything I had been keeping contained. In the weeks that proceeded, I hadn't taken the time to connect with Him, but I also hadn't taken the time to process my own state of heart or mind. Because prayer time is a sharing of hearts with the Lord, it is a time for us to come to not only know the Lord better, but also a time for us to know ourselves better.

## Practicing Private Prayer

> "Come to me, all you who labor and are burdened, and I will give you rest. Take my yoke upon you and learn from me, for I am meek and humble of heart; and you will find rest for yourselves."
> Matthew 11:28-29

A prayer is a conversation, which starts with a daily "Yes" to spending time with the Lord. Knowing my distractions, I now do the unthinkable. I, too, wake up before the kids. I wake up and spend time in prayer with the Lord. Maybe that sounds crazy to you, but personally, I know at 9 p.m. any private prayer time I have will be very short, and I will fall asleep before the *amen* hits my lips! But maybe you are a night owl and would find the night prayers to be a beautiful way to end your evening.

The important thing is to just try something and stick with it.

Try for a time when you are fresh and calm. It is hard to stay focused if you have 1,000 things running through your mind. But don't get discouraged. If you find your mind turning to the to-do list, invite the Holy Spirit in to order your day. You may find that He has something else He wants to direct you towards, and it is okay to explore that with Him.

My mind was particularly messy one week in prayer so I opened my hour with the rosary. It is not generally my favorite prayer, but working my way through the beads allowed the wheels in my mind to slow, my heart rate and breathing calmed, and I was then able to listen to the Lord, and share my heart with Him. It is hard to pray when you are stressed, so calm yourself before you really invite the Lord into prayer.

Start with ten minutes, and as it becomes possible, try to work up to a Holy Hour. Your daily schedules will change, and your prayer life will need to adapt. And it should change because spiritually you should be growing. What you did last year shouldn't be enough for you this year. If you say an Our Father before bed every night that is a good start. But don't leave it at that. God wants an intimate relationship with you.

And He doesn't want to wait until you have extra time.

Maybe you are at the point in your life where you enjoy waking up before anyone else and having that first cup of coffee in the silence of the kitchen while you read scripture and pray. My grandmother used to do that up to her last days. Maybe yours is a family Hail Mary as you pull away from the house each morning. Wherever you are starting today, I encourage you to recognize that as a starting point. Not the norm to just keep doing as though you are in maintenance mode.

## Problems in Prayer

Sometimes there may be insights in prayer, but other times it is a sharing of love and relationship without insight. I have the tendency to enter into prayer as an intellectual exercise, rather than as a sharing of heart. This can be dangerous because prayer is not an emotional or intellectual exercise.

It is relational.

It is allowing the Lord into our heart.

Often the best way for me to enter into that deeper relationship is to start with the Christmas List of requests. Doing this lets me unburden myself of my worries. I throw them in a messy heap on the Lord and then I can be more open with Him. I have gotten all the junk off the mind and heart, so now I can be more present to Him. It is a good starting place—

but if you limit your conversations to just the Christmas gift list of requests, you are limiting your intimacy with Him.

Unburden yourself. Let go of the emotions, not just the desires. Then listen.

There will be times of consolation where we feel His presence deeply. There will also be times of desolation however, when we struggle to hear His voice, to see His face, to feel His touch. In the times of consolation we should rejoice, knowing that we may sometimes experience desolation in prayer. In our time of desolation, we should maintain our routine, confident that in time He will give us the satisfaction of feeling His love. The practice of Ignatian spirituality encourages us to resist making changes when we find ourselves in a period of desolation, but rather to keep to the commitments made when we were in a period of consolation, and view the time as an opportunity to show strength of faith in perseverance.

Dryness in prayer does not mean it is unhelpful or pointless. We are to have persistence in prayer. Continue to talk to and with the Father, even when you have trouble hearing His voice. Let your ritual of prayer sustain you in these times.

In times of desolation in particular, it may be helpful to turn to scripture. Jesus is alive in the word. When your heart grows quiet to His voice, your mind can continue to explore His Word, His life, His teachings set down in sacred scripture. Times of desolation can be helped when we keep in mind that we pray to please God–not ourselves.

## PRACTICAL

*"We pray not to find self-fulfillment or self-satisfaction, but to please God."*
Philippe, 2008

I was a swimmer in college. I quickly learned that if I did the same set every day for a year I wouldn't get better. I needed to challenge myself, but I needed a good coach to help me.

Spiritually, maybe you need a coach too. Friends who share the faith can be a good addition to that spiritual workout. They can challenge you and introduce you to new ways to grow closer to the Lord. Another option, if you find yourself spinning your wheels a little, is to find a spiritual director.

The first place to start though is by providing yourself with some structured prayer time each day, and within that time, experiment with a variety of different types of prayer. The Liturgy of the Hours is based on times, but for some, another option can be to base our patterns of prayers on routine. I have built-in morning private prayer and daily mass into my routine because that is what works best for me. Others I know commit to praying for themselves or loved ones at whatever time of day aligns with when they were born, or just their birthday. Know someone who shares Jesus' birthday? At 12:25, pray for that person. Remember always that the goal of prayer is to experience an intimate encounter with the Lord.

*Are you striving for consistent daily encounters with your Father? How can you obtain that? Take some time now to jot down some concrete times where you can have prayer as part of your routine.*

_____

_____

_____

_____

Don't be afraid to try new things and don't be discouraged when something isn't working out right. Prayer is the best thing to try boldly because it is private! Take a risk. No one but God will know if you try and fail and try again! Simply strive to find what works for you. You will fail, we all do, so try and try again. Some people succeed with having prayer reminders on their phones. Others prefer hard copies of prayer or scripture around their home to serve as little reminders to pray. Maybe you are someone who would benefit from a prayer journal. Maybe you need organized prayer time like daily mass.

Your prayer life will look different from everyone else's prayer life.

Don't be discouraged; rather be assured that you are all on different journeys to the same Christ. Don't compare your prayer life to others. Prayer is relationship building–so by definition, *it is personal!* Start where you are and begin to improve, and keep your eyes on God. Your goal is to grow deeper in your understanding of God's will in your life as you live as His daughter. His relationship with someone else is none of your concern.

*What can you do to deepen your prayer experience? If nothing comes to mind immediately sit with this question for a few minutes and see if the Lord brings anything to mind for you.*

## Developing the Heart

Although rituals are important and some would say essential for perseverance in the spiritual life, ritual is not sufficient. St. Teresa of Avila was convinced that if one wanted to deepen her prayer life, she must bring her will into conformity with God's will. One must live the Gospel or as Fr. Dubay (1989) writes, "Do God's will from moment to moment throughout the day." When one lives the gospel in conformity with God's will, she is able to enter into a deeper or more advanced prayer life. This is the primary or basic Teresian principle for growth in the spiritual life. It cannot be achieved by merely following a prayer protocol.

Private prayer is essential to the spiritual life, but only talking to Jesus when you are alone at some self-appointed time is precisely the opposite of living a life of prayer. Living a life of prayer means turning your eyes heavenward when you find yourself frustrated, excited, or even just normal or so-so.

- It means keeping Him in your consciousness.
- It means asking the Lord for guidance when you have daily decisions to make.
- It means washing the dishes while you recite a Hail Mary or two.
- It means asking the Lord to bless the food you are preparing, the bodies who will wear the clothes you are washing, the people you meet in the stores.
- It means cultivating silence in your spaces, even for the briefest of moments.

God has the incredible ability to be with us always. He is the best friend Who never goes away. During the mass during the Doxology we hear the words of the priest "through Him, with Him and in Him." This is how we strive to live: Through Him, with Him, and in Him. It is a beautiful goal to strive for a level of reflectiveness and awareness of His presence in our day. We can't always sit in quiet meditation, but we can strive for oneness with the Lord in the everyday moments.

He is in the stillness.

He is in the wind.

He is in the pots and the pans.

He is in the laundry and the garden.

He is where our mind wanders and is found when we cast our gaze beyond the physical-when we look not with our eyes but with our hearts.

My favorite Saint, St. Teresa of Avila says, "Contemplative prayer in my opinion is nothing else than a close sharing between friends; it means taking time frequently to be alone with Him who we know loves us" (Catholic Church, 2709). Doesn't she make it sound so simple? It means sharing your day with Him and quieting your mind. It can be done in solitude, but it doesn't need to be. Prayer is about building a relationship with the Lord, and He is happy to be a part of the nitty-gritty, not just the quiet and the pretty.

Welcome the Lord into the nitty-gritty parts of your day.

The ability to live a prayerful life is a gift from God, not something to be taught. However, we can help each other learn how to receive the gift, and I sincerely hope you have begun to learn how to be more receptive to Him. His will gives us the grace to be His daughter, irrespective of our personal feelings, internal dispositions, or personal preparations (Philippe, 2008). To be His daughter means to desire to know Him and to allow ourselves to let Him father us, love us, heal us, guide us, and protect us.

*Lord, My Father,*
*You created me for a beautiful purpose in this world which only I can serve. Help me to align my will to Yours everyday through intentional prayer. Help me to hear Your voice in the silence. Let me feel Your hand in the crowd. Love me through my pain and let me walk closer to You each day with each breath I take. Only then will I best live out my unique and beautiful purpose in this world for which you have so carefully designed me.*
*I love You.*
*Amen.*

Chapter 10

## CONCLUSION

*"Each of us can fulfill in our life that for which we were created. We cannot be sure that we have the gifts needed for any other purpose... For God, in creating us, equipped us for the work for which He created us."*
Maturin, 2016

I can't stress it enough, sisters—we cannot know who we are fully until we come to see ourselves as God sees us: As His daughter. When we are able to recognize our unique gifts, to surrender the things that separate us from the Lord, and enter more deeply into a relationship with Him, we are able to grow in our understanding of how the Lord loves us and how we are uniquely designed to serve Him in this world.

This understanding changes *everything*.

Once we know what we have to give, know who we are striving to be, and recognize our strength and purpose comes from the Lord, we can approach the daily frustrations and challenges of life with holiness. This means we choose to give of ourselves, rather than merely reacting to the world, which constantly asks for more. We stop feeling as though we are giving up ourselves and rather learn to come into our true being, giving freely of the talents, gifts, and charisms we have been endowed with from the Lord.

We were created for a relationship with God. It is the reason we exist!! That is our unified purpose. This relationship was ruptured through original sin, but restored through the sacrifice of Jesus Christ. Jesus came to restore us to a relationship with God the Father. We have an opportunity to say yes to Jesus and the chance to be restored in relationship as daughters. He died and rose and now reigns eternally, that we may too live with Him in all eternity in Heaven.

The Lord loves us deeply and does not expect perfection from us. He meets us where we are and he desires a relationship with us. Holiness is walking with God, sharing our lives with Him, and letting Him help us.

All that is required is our "Yes."

It is a one-time "Yes," but it is also a continual "Yes." We commit our lives to Him, and then we renew that commitment every day as we serve with love and affection. We say "Yes" when we offer Him our day every morning before our feet hit the floor, or breathe in His peace before responding to the frustrations around us, or when we take time out everyday to better know Him in the Word, or when we say those Hail Marys as we watch our children playing at the park or riding their bikes down the path.

## CONCLUSION

The beautiful thing is, there are hundreds of ways every day to say "Yes" and grow closer to the Lord. It can be intimidating to take that first step towards developing a prayer life in the chaos, but it starts with a simple "Yes."

Believe me when I tell you—with intentionality and persistence, you can have a prayer life that helps you enter into an intense relationship with the Lord and helps you to foster a deeper sense of self and what it means to be His daughter. It's exactly what you were designed for.

It is only through prayer that we can grow in true wisdom, and it is wisdom that allows us to both persevere in suffering and grow in humility. Wisdom is the solution to embracing our suffering with joy. Wisdom provides us with protection against the destructiveness of self-worth that results from living a life of comparison rather than a life of holiness.

We all have different paths to salvation, but Jesus Christ is the one gate through which we all pass. God's desire is for us all to be with Him, our loving Father. The paths are filled with challenges of all sizes and these challenges give us the opportunity to grow in virtue and deeper understanding of what it means to be His daughter.

My prayer is that you will continue to draw near to the Father and know in a very real way His inexpressible, unrepeatable love for you—through the busyness, the distractions, the dry spells, the pain, the doubts—through all of it, believe that He delights endlessly in calling you "daughter."

# CITATIONS

♦ ♦

Ames, Mark-Mary. *Habits for Holiness.* West Chester: Ascension Press, 2021.

Augustine, of Hippo, Saint. *The Confessions of Saint Augustine.* London: Penguin Group, 1961.

Catholic Church. *Catechism of the Catholic Church.* 1st ed. Vatican: Libreria Editrice Vaticana, 1994.

Catholic Church. (1987). *Encyclical letter Redemptoris mater of the Supreme Pontiff John Paul II on the Blessed Virgin Mary in the life of the pilgrim Church.* Ottawa: Canadian Conference of Catholic Church.

Dubay, Thomas. *Fire Within.* San Francisco: Ignatius Press, 1989.

Gabriel. *Divine Intimacy: Meditations on the interior life for everyday of the liturgical year.* Rockford: Tan Books and Publishers, Inc, 1996.

Gorbachev, Mikhail. 2007. Speech delivered at Harvard University, Dec. 4, 2007. https://www.harvardmagazine.com/breaking-news/if-you-dont-move-forward-you-begin-move-backward.

Hart, Dolores. *The Ear of the Heart.* San Francisco: Ignatius, 2013.

# CITATIONS

*Holy Bible: The Catholic Journaling Bible.* The New American Bible Revised Edition. Huntington: Our Sunday Visitor Publishing, 2017.

Lawrence. *Practice of the Presence of God.* New Kensington: Whitaker House, 1982.

Lewis, C. S. *The Screwtape Letters.* New Jersey: Lord and King Associates, 1976.

Maturin, Basil. *Spiritual Guidelines for Souls Seeking God.* Manchester: Sophia Press, 2016.

Paul VI. *Evangelica Testificatio.* Apostolic Exhortation. Vatican: the Holy See. Vatican Website. Libreria Editrice Vaticana, 1971. https://www.vatican.va/content/paul-vi/en/apost_exhortations/documents/hf_p-vi_exh_19710629_evangelica-testificatio.html.

Philippe, Jacques. *Searching for and Maintaining Peace: A Small Treatise on Peace of Heart.* Strongsville: Scepter, 1991.

Philippe, Jacques. *Time with God.* Strongsville: Scepter, 2008.

Philippe, Jacques. *God's Peace.* Virtual Retreat, November 20-22, 2020.

Sarah, Robert Cardinal. *The Power of Silence: Against the dictatorship of noise.* San Francisco: Ignatius Press, 2016.

Teresa, of Avila, Saint. *The Interior Castle.* New York: Barnes and Noble, 2005.

Teresa, of Calcutta, Saint in C. Kelly-Gangi (Ed). *Mother Teresa: Her essential wisdom,* New York: Fall River Press, 2006.

# ACKNOWLEDGMENTS

♦ ♦

My heart is filled with gratitude for the friends and family who have helped me along this writing process.

To my husband Bob, so loving and patient, you never doubted that this was a project worthy of the time and dedication it required. Thank you for supporting me and always responding confidently that I could do this. You gave me faith and courage when I needed it–which ended up being rather frequently!

To Evan, Joshua, Ella and Juliette, who rarely grumbled when they realized that I had forgotten to start dinner, or we ran out of some essential food item, or when I requested quiet because my head was just too full of words that needed to be spilled out onto the pages.

To my mom and dad, for reading early drafts, commenting and correcting, supporting and encouraging me. You probably never thought you would still be editing my writing all these years later, but I am grateful for it all.

To my friends who offered support for the project: Sr. Maria Kim, for initially telling me years ago that I needed to write a book and giving me confidence that it would be published. Trish, for brainstorming early titles and always

## ACKNOWLEDGMENTS

checking in to see how things were going. Nell and Jenna, for being the first and last eyes on the project, and for giving me hope when I became discouraged. My spiritual directors and prayer warriors, you know who you are and I am so grateful for your prayers. Lastly, Mike and Claire, for seeing this through the final stages and getting it off the computer and into the hands of women ready to grow and more deeply discover their identity as daughters of the beloved Father.

# ABOUT THE AUTHOR

MaryRuth Hackett holds a PhD in Educational Psychology with a concentration on Lifespan development. Her interest in helping parents and families integrate the best of science, the depths of the Catholic faith, and the uniqueness of their individual gifts and parenting styles led to the blog Parenting With Peer Review, the popular Parenting Smarts Podcast, and opportunities to speak on parenting and family life to groups around the country.

Raised Protestant, her conversion to the Catholic Faith in 2006 allowed MaryRuth to further embrace the Church's timeless wisdom around authentic femininity. As the key to both personal wholeness and effective parenting, she has come to appreciate the need to strengthen a woman's identity as a daughter of God before anything else.

A regular contributor to Spiritualdirection.com and Blessed is She's books and devotionals, MaryRuth writes and teaches at the important intersection of faith and science, blending them both in the original harmony God intended.

## ABOUT THE AUTHOR

MaryRuth is a lifetime resident of Arizona where she lives with her husband and four children—all of whom provide plenty of practical experience to complement the theory and research that informs her work. When she's not writing, speaking, or wrangling children, you might find her enjoying a cup of coffee and some historical fiction or mapping out her next traveling adventure.

She would love to connect with readers online at maryruthhackett.com/